Other Books by Lee Jenkins

Permission to Forget: And Nine Other Root Causes of America's Frustration with Education

Improving Student Learning: Applying Deming's Quality Principles in Classrooms

Boot Camp for Leaders in K–12 Education: Continuous Improvement (with Lloyd Roettger and Caroline Roettger)

FROM SYSTEMS THINKING TO SYSTEMIC ACTION

48 KEY QUESTIONS TO GUIDE THE JOURNEY

Lee Jenkins

Published in partnership with the
American Association of School Administrators

Rowman & Littlefield Education
Lanham • New York • Toronto • Plymouth, UK

Published in partnership with
the American Association of School Administrators

Published in the United States of America
by Rowman & Littlefield Education
A Division of Rowman & Littlefield Publishers, Inc.
A wholly owned subsidary of The Rowman & Littlefield Publishing
Group, Inc.
4501 Forbes Boulevard, Suite 200, Lanham, Maryland 20706
www.rowmaneducation.com

Estover Road
Plymouth PL6 7PY
United Kingdom

British Library Cataloguing in Publication Information Available

Library of Congress Cataloging-in-Publication Data

Jenkins, Lee, 1942–
  From systems thinking to systemic action: 48 key questions to guide the
journey / Lee Jenkins.
      p. cm.
  Includes bibliographical references and index.
  ISBN-13: 978-1-57886-819-3 (cloth : alk. paper)
  ISBN-10: 1-57886-819-X (cloth : alk. paper)
  ISBN-13: 978-1-57886-820-9 (pbk. : alk. paper)
  ISBN-10: 1-57886-820-3 (pbk. : alk. paper)
  eISBN-10: 1-57886-900-5
  eISBN-13: 978-1-57886-900-8
  1. School management and organization—United States. 2. School
improvement programs—United States. 3. Educational leadership—United
States. I. Title.

LB2805.J42 2008
371.2'07—dc22

                                                          2008007141

∞™ The paper used in this publication meets the minimum requirements
of American National Standard for Information Sciences—Permanence of
Paper for Printed Library Materials, ANSI/NISO Z39.48-1992.
Manufactured in the United States of America.

CONTENTS

LIST OF FIGURES   vii

PREFACE   ix

INTRODUCTION   xiii

    PART I: THE OVERALL SYSTEM

    1   VALUES   3

    2   CONSTANCY OF PURPOSE   19

    PART II: THE PEOPLE

    3   DEVELOPMENT OF PEOPLE   37

    4   COMMUNICATION   55

    5   SAFETY   71

    6   PERSONNEL OFFICE   77

PART III: THE PHYSICAL ASSETS

7   FINANCE   89

8   OPERATIONS AND BUILDINGS   97

PART IV: THE STUDENT LEARNING

9   PROCESS (FORMATIVE) DATA   107

10   RESULTS (SUMMATIVE) DATA   121

11   CURRICULUM   137

12   INSTRUCTION   145

CHARTING YOUR PROGRESS   161

AFTERWORD   163

THE 48-ITEM FINAL   167

THE 48 QUESTIONS   171

APPENDIX A: PERMISSION FOR
    INTERDISCIPLINARY ASSIGNMENT   177

APPENDIX B: THE KEY PROBLEMS   179

BIBLIOGRAPHY   181

INDEX   185

ABOUT THE AUTHOR   189

LIST OF FIGURES

Figure 1.1.   Fishbone   15

Figure 5.1.   Pareto Chart for Middle School Discipline Issues   74

Figure 9.1.   Student Run Chart   111

Figure 9.2.   Class Run Chart   111

Figure 9.3.   Scatter Diagram   114

Figure 9.4.   L to J Histogram   115

Figure 10.1.   Chamber of Commerce Chart   125

Figure 10.2.   Cecil County Radar Chart Figure   126

Figure 10.3.   Correlation Chart   129

Figure 10.4.   Pareto Chart from Cottonwood, Arizona, Schools   130

Figure 10.5.   Grade 3 Control Chart for Seventeen Schools   132

PREFACE

The foundation for *From Systems Thinking to Systemic Action* is rooted in the teachings of W. Edwards Deming. The first section of the book is a concise description of systems thinking; the second section contains 48 key questions, divided into twelve chapters. The questions are written to guide leaders as they transform their systems. Leaders are admonished to build quality into their systems and not attempt to inspect quality into their systems. *From Systems Thinking to Systemic Action* is written to assist leaders on this journey from systems thinking to systems action.

Dr. Deming loved to ask his audiences the question, "Who has the most influence over a ship crossing the ocean?" After rejecting the answers captain, navigator, and engine room operator, he stated that the person with the most control over the ship is the person that designed the ship. It will never perform better than it was designed to perform. Thus, I would say that the person who took the bell-shaped curve from science and misapplied it to education probably has more control over today's education than any current practicing educator. If only a few can succeed in every classroom, then no matter how talented the captain (school superintendent/director), the navigator (principal), or the engine room operator (teacher), the students cannot all excel. The school cannot perform better than it was designed to perform. "The system itself has prevented even the most talented and industrious among us from seeing this pronounced gap between poor and effective practices."[1]

From Systems Thinking to Systemic Action is all about the design. The key questions are written to assist in both understanding current design and potential re-design. Thomas Freese wrote, "He who asks the question has the power."[2] My desire is to provide leaders with the power to truly effect lasting improvement. This power comes not by bullying people, but by improving the system.

One example of a system change that could influence millions of children is the school calendar. Now, the system in almost, if not all, U.S. states is that each school district is allowed to establish its own calendar. However, think about the possibility of bringing together representatives of schools and youth organizations in each state. This group establishes the state school calendar. The understanding is that if school districts will adopt this universal calendar, the youth organizations will commit to offering activities for young people on these nonschool days. Think about the millions of lives that would be enhanced over a few years with this one system change. The private schools could participate in the calendar, and homeschooled students could participate in the events scheduled all over each state.

Even though I believe great good could come from the school calendar system change, my aim in this preface is not to discuss calendars but to provide an example of how change to a system can have a profound impact upon the lives of students, parents, employees, and school board members.

At the end of the twelve chapters is a blank graph for charting progress. Readers can, after reading each chapter, shade in their assessment of their school district/divison.[3] Since no school system is perfect, it is expected this book can provide planning direction for future system improvement. As the dodecagon is studied, it will be obvious that some of the aspects of this book are about current operations, but most are about the future, when in all likelihood some other, yet-to-be-appointed leader will gain from current planning and leading.

"Western managers generally believe their poor performance in the global marketplace is due to factors that are out of their control. This belief provides them a basis for rationalizing their disinclination to make fundamental changes."[4] Educators are tempted to blame society and poor legislation and thus be disinclined to make fundamental changes. Others do not know what the fundamental changes are, so they use their power to make surface changes. Neither surface changes nor disinclination will improve the schools. The fundamental changes described in this book will bring about the improvement so desperately needed.

NOTES

1. Mike Schmoker, *Results Now* (Alexandria, VA: Association for Supervision and Curriculum Development, 2006), 4.

2. Thomas A. Freese, *Secrets of Question Based Selling* (Naperville, IL: Sourcebooks, 2000), 171.

3. Districts in the United States; divisions in Canada. Throughout this book I use the U.S. term "district"; I hope this is not confusing to Canadian readers who work in "divisions."

4. Russell Ackoff, *The Democratic Corporation* (New York: Oxford University Press, 1994), xi.

INTRODUCTION

The culture is the complete collection of an organization's processes, customers, employees, suppliers, results, decision making, and machines. Some of the processes are in policy, some in job descriptions, some in law, and many in past practice. Usually the culture is composed of numerous disconnected parts. This book is about continually moving from these disconnected parts to a coherent, well-constructed system. Recently I received an e-mail asking, "Why do hot dogs come in packages of ten and hot dog buns come in packages of eight?" This simple question can help the reader understand the purpose of systems thinking and what must be accomplished over and over to create school districts that operate as a system instead of as a collection of parts.

W. Edwards Deming divided systems thinking into four components. He said leaders need not be experts in any of the four but must have enough knowledge of them to lead well. The four are

- Appreciation for a system
- Knowledge about variation
- Theory of knowledge (epistemology)
- Psychology[1]

The purpose of this primer is to provide theoretical background in a very brief manner. Numerous books on the market can provide details. Since this book's purpose is to provide readers with practical suggestions for systemic action, a minimal approach to systemic thinking is appropriate. Readers will observe in each of the 48 questions that compose the body of this book elements of all four system components.

The purpose of the 48 questions is to provide application knowledge. When people are armed with only systems theory knowledge, two events occur: (1) people ask what they should do with all of this theory or (2) leaders teach the theory to their employees and expect them to figure out what to do with the systems theory. Neither is helpful to the employees or the organization.

Armed with only the 48 questions, people will push back and say they do not need these questions to operate their school system. *From Systems Thinking to Systemic Action* is the combination of both the why and the how. These questions and narratives have the power to positively impact the lives of numerous students, employees, and parents.

Deming writes that the four components of profound knowledge are necessary to understand a system. They cannot be separated. They interact with each other. "One need not be eminent in any part nor in all four parts in order to understand it and apply it."[2]

48 KEY CONCEPTS IN SYSTEMS THINKING

Appreciation of a System

1. "A system is a network of interdependent components that work together to accomplish the aim of the system."[3] The twelve chapters of this book are written separately. However, each system networks with the other systems; all are interdependent.
2. Systems must have an aim. "The first characteristic of a system is that it has a clearly defined and articulated aim. Absent

an aim there is no system."[4] Let's take social studies instruction, for example. Because there is no overall aim for social studies instruction from grades K–12, there is no social studies system in most school districts.

3. "A system must be managed. It will not manage itself. Left to themselves in the Western world, components become selfish, competitive, independent profit centers, and thus destroy the system."[5] The secret to having a successful system is cooperation between components.

4. Management of a system "requires knowledge of the interrelationships between all components within the system and the people that work in it."[6] School superintendents and their school boards are required to spend much of their time managing these interrelationships.

5. The ideal aim creates a "better life for everyone."[7] When issues are being deliberated, the aim must be to find a decision that is better for students, employees, and the community. For example, when an English teacher can spend 50 percent less evening/weekend time scoring papers *and* the students write better, we have created a better life for everyone.

6. One portion of the system cannot suboptimize the system, meaning that one portion of the system must not win at the expense of other aspects of the system. Leaders must always balance the competing demands of various segments of the school system. Legislators must temper their desires to have one component of the school system continually win at the expense of other components of the school district.[8]

7. In order for a system to be competitive, the management and employees must cooperate inside the organization.[9] We must not foster competition between students but encourage all of the students to cooperate in order for their school to win. The ideal "win" for a school system is to outperform all prior students. The elementary principal reports that these graduating fifth graders are the best-prepared students ever sent on to the middle school. The middle-school principal sends the

best-prepared students ever to high school, and the high-school principal, at graduation, says, "Note in the program all of the areas in which this class is better prepared than prior classes. Further, all of you juniors in the audience tonight, we are asking all of you to cooperate with each other so that I can say one year from now that you are the best-prepared class ever."

8. The components of a system are equipment, materials, suppliers, processes, customers, redesign process, and results.[10] Education may use slightly different terms, but the components are the same. For example, hospitals call their customers patients, athletic teams call their customers fans, and schools call their customers students and parents. Schools may change the terminology to better communicate but must not overlook a component.

9. When things go wrong, almost always the problem is the system. Deming estimated that the problem was the system from 94 to 97 percent of the time. My book *Permission to Forget: And Nine Other Root Causes of America's Frustration with Education* is an attempt to identify the 94 to 97 percent.[11]

10. If we want better results, we must improve the system. We must find a why instead of spending all of our time attempting to find a who. For example, if 100 percent inspection of all student papers produced quality work, this book would be unnecessary. However, the system currently in place is not producing the desired quality, so a process change is necessary if different results are desired.[12]

11. It takes fourth-generation management to lead a system. MBO (management by objective) is third generation and is inadequate. Teamwork is essential.[13]

12. The person with the most control over the organization is the person who designed the processes. The person who designed a system allowing students to cram and forget (even though this person is probably not alive today) has more control over education that most of the people currently working in the field. "The turning point for the Japanese was when they

shifted from detecting poor quality to preventing poor quality."[14] This shift in education thinking would be a major system design change. "Estimates show that it's ten times more expensive to correct a problem than to prevent it."[15]

Psychology

1. Ranking harms people. Awards assemblies are really a ranking activity. They motivate the 15 percent who receive the rewards and demotivate the other 85 percent. No parents send their children to school to be "losers" so other people's children can be "winners." We must find ways to honor all students for their strengths and interests.

2. There are two types of motivation: intrinsic and extrinsic. People often defend their use of extrinsic motivation by describing the most difficult of cases and the extreme need for extrinsic motivation for these individuals. Maybe it is necessary; I am not a psychologist. However, I observe that extrinsic motivation is applied to all students in schools. It starts in kindergarten with stickers and ends with grades. The 11,700 incentives (5 per day, for 180 school days, for 13 years) that students receive are not working.[16]

3. One is born with a natural inclination to learn.[17] Almost all students still possess this desire to learn when they enter kindergarten.

4. Leaders possess three attributes: knowledge, power, and personality.[18] Teachers have knowledge, power, and personality. Administrators have knowledge, power, and personality. School board members have knowledge, power, and personality. Everyone wants their bosses to use knowledge first, personality second, and last of all power.

5. Children are most like adults in their feelings and least like adults in their thinking. From university courses, educators learned about the "least like adults in their thinking" from Jean Piaget's research. However, the "most like us in their feelings" part was left out. If educators forget the first part,

students are frustrated; if they forget the second part, students are disenfranchised.

6. It is not the responsibility of educators to motivate children. They come to kindergarten already motivated. Thus, it is the responsibility of educators to determine what is causing the loss of motivation and stop such practices. "It is the controlling intent of rewards that sabotages their attempts to motivate others, destroying the very motivation they had been intending to promote."[19]

7. "Self-motivation, rather than external motivation, is at the heart of creativity, responsibility, healthy behavior, and lasting change."[20]

8. "People who were asked to do a particular task but allowed the freedom of having some say in how to do it were more fully engaged by the activity . . . than people who were not treated as unique individuals."[21]

9. "Kage found that the use of evaluative quizzes to motivate learning led to lowered intrinsic motivation and to poorer performance on the final examination than did the self-monitored, nonevaluative quizzes."[22]

10. "Rewards can be used as a way to express appreciation, but the more they are used as motivators, the more likely it is that they will have negative effects."[23]

11. "To be intrinsically motivated, people need to perceive themselves as competent and autonomous (self-governing); they need to feel that they are effective and self-determining. Someone else's opinion does not do the trick."[24]

12. Basic human needs: "autonomy, competence, and relatedness."[25]

Variation

1. The only reason people invented statistics was to understand variation. If no variation, no need for statistics.

2. There are two types of variation: special and common.[26] For example, in a fifth-grade classroom students reading like av-

erage fourth-, fifth-, and sixth-grade students are examples of common variation. Special variation would be reading like an average first- or eleventh-grade student while in fifth grade.

3. "There are two mistakes frequently made in attempts to improve results, both costly. Mistake 1. To react to an outcome as if it came from a special cause, when actually it came from common causes of variation. Mistake 2. To treat an outcome as if it came from common causes of variation, when actually it came from special causes."[27]

4. The bell curve, apparent in science, has been greatly misused in education. The bell curve is for the middle of the course. A bell curve at the end of the course is a sign of teacher failure, because some students in every course can teach themselves. Give a group of students only textbooks and computers, but no teacher, and a bell curve is what will occur. Give students a great teacher and the course will end in a J curve.[28]

5. Process data is during the school year, and results data is at the end of the year. Sometimes educators use the terms formative and summative instead of the generic terms.[29]

6. Data with one or two data points is useless. Apparent differences are due to luck or the system. The articles in the newspaper that have only one or two years of data must be replaced with trend data over five years or more. Otherwise save the ink. Legislative and other leaders must resist the temptation to alter the annual exams every couple of years because they damage the trends, making all the data impotent.

7. Disaggregation is helpful in management of organizations; aggregation is powerful in leading the organization. Both are needed.

8. PGA is a useful mnemonic device for classifying statistical tools. P is for perception, G is for graph, and A is for analysis. Education abounds with perceptions and sometimes has analysis. The G is usually missing. It is the powerful use of graphs that should be the focus of the master's degree statistical course; the doctoral statistical course can stay with the analysis.

9. Statistical control means that the variation in the future is predictable.[30] Most schools are in statistical control. Calculate the average number of dropouts for the past five years. Almost certainly, that is the number of dropouts from future classes. Calculate the average number of discipline referrals, the average number of Fs, the number of students with excessive absences, and so on. The future can be predicted with great accuracy. "Statistics deals with two areas: the past and the future. We use statistics to summarize past events so we can understand them. We then use this summary to make predictions about the future."[31]

10. "Use of data requires also understanding of the distinction between enumerative studies and analytic problems."[32] In chapter 10, the five graphs for results data can be classified as follows: The chamber-of-commerce chart and the radar chart are enumerative; the correlation, Pareto, and control charts are analytical.

11. The three basic classroom graphs, run chart, scatter diagram, and histogram, are enumerative (chapter 9).[33]

12. Tally marks and the Pareto chart are the major item analysis tools for the classroom.

Epistemology

1. Management is prediction. Every decision by administrators, teachers, and school board members is a prediction. "We predict that if we make this decision, rather than this decision, the future will be better."

2. Test theories, not kids. Involve the students in the experiment. Let them know that you have a hypothesis that a particular strategy will help them learn and then observe together to see if the hypothesis was correct.

3. The graphing of data provides insights not apparent from raw data. When people are overwhelmed with numbers they cannot see what is occurring. Insights generate hypotheses, which generate learning if an experiment is conducted.

4. Experience is not the best teacher; testing theories is the best teacher. Many times teachers give credit to experience when actually their improvement occurred because they tested out several theories until they came across what worked for them.[34]

5. It takes only one example contrary to a theory to require one to revisit the theory. "A thousand examples won't prove a theory. A single example can disprove a theory."[35] For example, we have a theory that punishment improves behavior. Every school has a student immune to punishment. While punishment may work for the majority, it does not work for all. Thus, educators must continue to refine the theory. Also, high schools have a theory that ninth graders are more likely to graduate from high school if they take all required courses. Maybe this is true for most, but not all. So, what should the theory be?

6. Ask why at least five times to find the root causes of a problem. The root cause lies beyond the source.[36] Once the root cause is discovered, it will be somebody's pet project or process. Ouch.

7. The curriculum in schools is divided into two major categories: what students are to know and what they are to perform. Continuous improvement processes can reduce the time necessary for students to learn the "know" component of the curriculum, leaving more time for the "can do."

8. Leaders are to create more leaders: student leaders, teacher leaders, administrator leaders, food service leaders, secretary leaders, and so on.

9. Plan-Do-Study-Act is a learning cycle. The most important aspect of "plan" is baseline data; then comes the experiment. If the study of the results indicates an improvement, then people must take action to make the improvement stick.

10. Instead of management decisions, we need many more management hypotheses. This is an admission that nobody knows for sure the best decision, but we have to land on one hypothesis. For example, what is the best schedule for a high

school? What are we attempting to accomplish, and then what hypotheses do we want to test first?[37]

11. Interest is the major determination of successful learning. Adults and children can learn what they are interested in. The struggle to learn is actually the struggle to understand. Once understood, learning is very quick.

12. Standards and accountability do not mean that creativity and joy must be removed from the learning process.

NOTES

1. W. Edwards Deming, *The New Economics for Industry, Government, and Education* (Cambridge, MA: Massachusetts Institute of Technology, Center for Advanced Engineering Study, 1993), 93.

2. Deming, 93.

3. Deming, 50.

4. Lee Jenkins, Lloyd O. Roettger, and Caroline Roettger, *Boot Camp for Leaders in K–12 Education: Continuous Improvement* (Milwaukee, WI: Quality Press, 2007), 5.

5. Deming, 50.

6. Deming, 50.

7. Deming, 52.

8. Jenkins, Roettger, and Roettger, 110.

9. Jenkins, Roettger, and Roettger, 127.

10. Deming, 58.

11. Lee Jenkins, *Permission to Forget: And Nine Other Root Causes of America's Frustration with Education* (Milwaukee, WI: Quality Press, 2005).

12. Jenkins, Roettger, and Roettger, 105–6.

13. Jenkins, Roettger, and Roettger, 9–10.

14. Warren T. Ha, ed., *The Book of Statistical Process Control* (Cincinnati, OH: Zontec Press, 2002), 3.

15. Ha, 10.

16. Jenkins, Roettger, and Roettger, 99–100.

17. Lee Jenkins, *Improving Student Learning: Applying Deming's Quality Principles in Classrooms*, 2nd ed. (Milwaukee, WI: Quality Press, 2003), 129.

18. Deming, 116.

19. Edward L. Deci and Richard Flaste, *Why We Do What We Do* (New York: Penguin, 1995), 38.

20. Deci and Flaste, 9.

21. Deci and Flaste, 34.

22. Deci and Flaste, 49.

23. Deci and Flaste, 55.

24. Deci and Flaste, 86.

25. Deci and Flaste, 98.

26. Ha, 13.

27. Deming, 99.

28. Jenkins, Roettger, and Roettger, 49.

29. Jenkins, Roettger, and Roettger, 65–73, 133–46.

30. William J. Latzko and David M. Saunders, *Four Days with Dr. Deming* (Reading, MA: Addison-Wesley, 1995), 39.

31. Ha, 19.

32. Deming, 100.

33. Jenkins, Roettger, and Roettger, 65–73.

34. Jenkins, *Permission to Forget*, 63–65.

35. Latzko and Saunders, 41.

36. Jeffrey K. Liker, *The Toyota Way* (New York: McGraw-Hill, 2004), 253.

37. Jenkins, *Permission to Forget*, 65–67.

I

THE OVERALL SYSTEM

1

VALUES

In order for the school board to be successful, the superintendent must be successful. In order for the school superintendent to be successful, the district as a whole must stop blaming and search for root causes of problems.

VISION, PURPOSE, CORE VALUES, AND BELIEFS

Vision, purpose, core values, and beliefs abound in education. These deeply held beliefs and aspirations inspire countless educators to pursue the best for our next generation. *From Systems Thinking to Systemic Action* is all about systems thinking and systemic action. Certain values are essential in order to harness the power of systems thinking. These values are not contrary to most other values held by educators, but they form the foundation for system leadership.

"Vision is the What—the picture of the future we seek to create . . . Purpose or mission is the Why . . . Core values answer the question, 'How do we want to act, consistent with our mission, along the path toward achieving our vision?'"[1] Beliefs are the collection of all three—vision, purpose, and core values. Throughout this book, I will be speaking to all of these three plus many practical ideas for implementation of the beliefs. All of the chapters hinge, however, on the answer to the first question.

Vision, Purpose, Core Values, and Beliefs Question 1

Do the superintendent and board accept the belief that 94 to 97 percent of the school district's issues are system problems?

If leaders cannot accept the basic premise of systems thinking, that 94 to 97 percent of the organization's problems are caused by the system,[2] then this book will be of no help. Top officials must truly understand that "No amount of care or skill in workmanship can overcome fundamental faults of the system."[3] It would be very easy for readers to assume that I am speaking of the system created by the legislature. I am not. I am speaking of the local school system. Yes, there are societal problems, and yes, there are numerous legislative problems, but this book is about the local school system. Dr. W. Edwards Deming taught that when things go wrong in Japan, leaders ask why until they find out why, and in the United States, leaders ask why until they find a who.[4] Leaders must ask why, why, why, why, and why some more until they uncover the root causes of their problems. Rarely is the problem caused by lazy, incompetent, or clueless employees; the problems are caused by unanticipated results of a prior, seemingly logical, decision. Peter Senge states this so precisely when he says, "Today's problems come from yesterday's 'solutions.'"[5] He further states, "Once I saw the problem as structurally caused, I began to look at what I could do, rather than at what 'they had done.'"[6] "Quality is determined by top management. It can not be delegated."[7]

How can leaders know if a problem falls within the 3 to 6 percent that are truly people problems? The best way is to ask if the problem occurs over and over. If so, it is a system problem. The high-school dropout issue is an example of a reoccurring problem. Following Dr. Deming's estimates of people versus system problems, one can ascertain that 3 to 6 percent of the dropouts are caused by the students themselves and the rest are the result of the system.

I was discussing education with a state legislator who served on his state's education committee. He asked me, "Why are educators so defensive when we pass new education laws?" I asked him if he had heard of Edwards Deming. He replied, "Yes." I then asked him if he had heard that Dr. Deming estimated that 94 to 97 percent of the problems of all organizations are caused by the system and the remaining problems by people making errors. He replied that he had not heard this about Dr. Deming. I then stated, "That's why we educators are so defensive. If you passed laws to fix the system, we'd help you fix the system, but you pass laws to fix us. Of course we are defensive."

It would be very easy for educators to read this and say, "Right on! Those legislators need to understand." However, educators are guilty of the same blame game. We just blame different people. Superintendents blame the board and the union. Principals blame the "Pink Palace" or whatever the district office is labeled. Teachers blame students, parents, and administrators. Students blame teachers, and nothing improves.

The belief that 94 to 97 percent of a school district's problems are caused by the system is the crucial first step in moving from blaming to systems thinking. My book *Permission to Forget: And Nine Other Root Causes of America's Frustration with Education* is an attempt to outline at least ten of the system problems infecting education.[8] The title, *Permission to Forget*, is really a synonym for cramming. No current educator established a formal policy that students have permission to forget. However, that is the reality of spelling tests, chapter tests, and all other assessments of short-term memory. "Permission to forget" is just one example of a system problem.

I have interviewed hundreds of teacher applicants and asked, "Why do you want to be a teacher?" None ever answered, "I want to help children with their short-term memory." However, once teachers are hired, many of the grades, beginning with first-grade spelling, are based upon short-term crammed memory. The teachers are performing the exact opposite of what they believe. Why? It is the power of the system. The leaders who remove cramming as an option from their K–12 or university system have done more for their staff and students than any amount of blame could accomplish.

In the Dover-Eyota School District (Minnesota), the science department is determined to remove permission to forget. The students are responsible in tenth-grade biology for all key concepts from seventh grade through biology. In the district's first year of taking away permission to forget, students in tenth grade were only responsible for biology key concepts and scored an average of 82 percent correct. The second year, students had to remember both ninth-grade and tenth-grade science; the third year of implementation, eighth-, ninth-, and tenth grades; and now students are expected to remember four grades of science concepts. The data from Dover-Eyota shows that taking away permission to forget is not easy. Students learn about cramming through first-grade spelling, and it is tough to change their minds in high school. However, the Dover-Eyota science department is determined that students in the twenty-first century can actually remember what they were taught.

Their results are

Year	Expectation	Percent Correct in Grade 10
2003	Grade 10 biology	81%
2004	Grades 9 and 10	72%
2005	Grades 8, 9, and 10	70%
2006	Grades 7, 8, 9, and 10	55%
2007	Grades 7, 8, 9, and 10	78%

It would have been so easy to give up in 2006 and say permission to forget is bigger than us, but the staff did not give up; when the system changes, the students will change.

In order for a district to answer yes to question 1 under values, purpose, core values, and beliefs, the leaders must commit themselves to asking why, why, why, why, and why when problems occur. All must disavow blaming.

Vision, Purpose, Core Values, and Beliefs Question 2

Once a school system can attest to the fact that most accept the basic premise of systems thinking, it is ready to ask the second question: "Has the organization disavowed the use of force, intimidation, manipulation, or incentives to achieve its goals?"[9] When leaders use force, intimidation, manipulation, and incentives to "motivate" their staffs, they are saying loudly that they do not have a clue how to fix this problem. And since they do not have the knowledge to solve the issue, they fall back on inappropriate use of power. In the preface of his latest book, written at age ninety-two, Edwards Deming wrote, "This book is for people who are living under the tyranny of the prevailing style of management."[10] He further writes, "Most people imagine that this style of management has always existed, and is a fixture. Actually, it is a modern invention."[11] Clearly, the use of force intimidation, embarrassment, and incentives are the prevailing style of management. The list of four is from John Maxwell, who lists seven ways people wield influence over others. The list is from worst to best. The last three on the list are "persuasion, energizing others, and honor/serve."[12]

Bosses who ascribe to blaming as opposed to systems thinking make these statements:

1. "You better solve this problem by this date, or bad things will happen." (force)
2. In front of many employees, they say, "Lee, why cannot you fix this issue; other school systems do not have this problem." (intimidation)
3. "We have others who would love to have your job." (manipulation)
4. "I have set aside some money for a bonus for those who solve this issue." (incentives)

When teachers do not have the knowledge to solve a student learning problem, they often rely upon the same four wrongheaded tools.

1. They rely on force, threatening a failing grade, detention, and suspension.
2. They use intimidation with invidious compliments (intimidation by praising one student in front of the whole class to make

the rest of the class envious). Sometimes they post grades in rank order, or even worse, hand out the exams in rank order from best to worst grade. Either way is classic management by intimidation.

3. They manipulate the system so that the struggling students are out of their classroom through various means, including special education, removal for bad behavior, parent request to have child removed, or ability grouping (child goes to somebody else for instruction).

4. The most common unsatisfactory method is incentives. Students receive over 10,000 incentives from K–12. "The effect of incentive pay is numbers and the loss of focus on the aim."[13] The effect of incentives in school is the prize or grade, not the aim: learning.

When administrators do not have the knowledge to improve their schools and school districts they:

1. Threaten job loss. (force)
2. Say, "If ___ school can meet its annual goals, why can't you?" or hand out at the principals' meetings ranked scores from all of the schools. (intimidation)
3. Move all of the low-performing students to independent study and give the independent study program a different school locator, thus assuring themselves that these students do not appear on their accountability report. (manipulation)
4. Go to business leaders in the community asking for money to use as cash bonuses for improved test scores. (incentives)

These four behaviors are at the root of much tension between some school superintendents and their school board members. If a school superintendent leads his/her school district with persuasion, enabling others, and honor/serving and a newly elected board member points out a problem within the school system, the school superintendent may be considered weak for not using force, intimidation, manipulation, and incentives to solve the problem. This is especially true if the newly elected board member has used force, intimidation, manipulation, and incentives to amass wealth. What this newly elected board member does not realize is "We will rise to our feet from fear, but it takes hope to keep us standing for the long term."[14] Further, "whenever there is fear, there will be wrong figures."[15] Another word for describing these behaviors is bullying. At Toyota, "Advancement of business performance by the parent company through bullying suppliers is totally alien to the spirit of the Toyota Production System."[16]

When leaders advocate incentives for employees, they are unintentionally saying, "I have no clue how to improve this system, but my lazy employees know how to bring about the needed improvement. Incentives will pry loose this withheld knowledge and all will be well." Joel Klein is making such an unintentional admission when advocating merit pay for increased test scores.[17] Further, New York City already has many, many self-motivated educators. "People with a sense of their own vision and commitment would naturally reject efforts of a leader to 'get them committed.'"[18]

Educators are often pressured by business leaders to use incentives to create better student learners. Business wants educators to believe their incentive systems work. However, Collins "found no systematic pattern linking executive compensation to the process of going from good to great. The evidence simply does not support the idea that the specific structure of executive compensation acts as a key lever in taking a company from good to great."[19] America's schools are already good, so why would business leaders, who hire Collins to speak at their conferences and to their employees, continue to not listen to his research? He writes further, "The good-to-great companies understood a simple truth: the right people will do the right things and deliver the best results they're capable of, regardless of the incentive system."[20]

Deming quotes a company's goals and objectives:

"1. Provide systems of reward that recognize superior performance, innovation, extraordinary care and commitment.
2. Create and maintain stimulating and enjoyable work environment, with the aim to attract, develop, and retain self-directed, talented people.

These two goals are incompatible. Goal 1 will induce conflict and competition between people, a sure road to demoralization. It will take the joy out of work, and will thus defeat Goal 2, however noble it be."[21]

Deci and Flaste describe what happens with the four negative approaches: "self motivation, rather than external motivation, is at the heart of creativity, responsibility, healthy behavior, and lasting change. External cunning or pressure can sometimes bring about compliance, but with compliance comes negative consequences, including the urge to defy."[22] They write further, "Intrinsic motivation is associated with richer experience, better conceptual understanding, greater creativity, and improved problem solving . . . Not only do controls undermine intrinsic motivation and engagement with activities but—and here is a bit of bad news for people focused on the bottom line—they have clearly detrimental effects on performance of any tasks that require creativity, conceptual understanding, or flexible problem solving."[23] This may help explain why schools are successful with reading decoding and math computation but struggle with reading comprehension and math problem solving.

One reason why question 2 is so important is "once you have begun to use rewards to control people, you can not easily go back."[24] I have worked with many teachers across the United States who have successfully "gone back" to intrinsic motivation, even in high school, with the process I described in *Improving Student Learning*.[25] Students will make the adjustment, but Deci and Flaste's adverb *easily* is certainly true.

I estimated earlier that U.S. students receive over 10,000 incentives in their K–12 education. This number is arrived at by multiplying 5 incentives per day times 180 school days times 13 years. In elementary schools, incentives are stickers, marbles in a jar, and popcorn parties, and in secondary school incentives are more food, videos, and grades. "When children are given rewards such as toys and money for doing well in school, music, and sports, they learn to expect rewards for good performance. As they become adults, their desire for tangible reward begins to govern action. They are now extrinsically motivated. They come to rely on the world to provide things to make them feel good. They will often work hard to earn lots of money, only to find in middle age that their work has no meaning."[26] In the simplest of terms, "Rewards motivate people to work for rewards."[27]

All four of these negative techniques can be classified under the use of fear. "The power of fear underlies negative visions. The power of aspiration drives positive visions. Fear can produce extraordinary changes in short periods, but aspiration endures as a continuing source of learning and growth."[28]

At this point, it is important to distinguish between incentives and celebrations. An incentive is a bribe used to motivate others, and a celebration is merely a thank you. The celebration can be individual or for a group. "Rewards and recognition are important, but as the research has clearly shown . . . when rewards or awards are used as a means of motivating people, they are likely to backfire."[29] I'll use food as an example to distinguish the difference. A teacher who says, "Everyone who learns their multiplication tables gets to come to the popcorn party," is clearly bribing using incentives. However, another teacher can say, "Today I brought popcorn for all of you just to say thanks for all of your hard work on the multiplication tables. I probably won't bring popcorn again, but I am so pleased with your work that I can't help myself." The difference is not subtle; one teacher is using power to control and the other is honoring students. One approach replaces intrinsic with extrinsic motivation and one encourages intrinsic motivation. I find, however, that over 90 percent of the celebrations with process data, described in chapter 9, do not involve food or anything that costs money.

The school district that can answer yes to question 2 does not use force, intimidation, manipulation, or incentives to reach its goals. But shouldn't force be used sometimes? The answer is yes, rarely. Appropriate uses of force are when there is 80 to 85 percent agreement for a new process and force may be necessary to have the full power of implementation. For example, a school system is working on payroll errors. The errors are coming in from schools into the payroll office. One school pilots a new process, and errors are cut down dramatically. Other schools volunteer to use the new practice with similar results. One school is remaining, and the secretary refuses to adopt the new practice. Force may be necessary, as a last resort. Another appropriate use of force is in the 3 to 6 percent of the cases where the employee is in the wrong profession. Applying force to the faculty as a whole is totally inappropriate, but when all else fails, in certain situations, force is required.

Vision, Purpose, Core Values, and Beliefs Question 3

If an organization can answer yes to question 2, then the third question is, "Does the organization have in place structures to regularly remove barriers and waste?" Barrier removal is not an afterthought.

Once an organization accepts the belief that 94 to 97 percent of the problems are caused by the system and disavows force, manipulation, intimidation, and incentives, problems all go away. Wrong. Problems are always present. However, if a school system asks, "Why do we still have this problem? We have great employees and students. We are using persuasion, we energize others, we honor and serve our employees and students, but are still facing many of the same issues," the next step is barrier removal.

What is causing our difficulty? What is the root cause of the problem? The organization must be willing to ask the hard questions about its practices to remove barriers to everyone's success. The school system must be willing to listen to parents and students to find out what precisely the barriers are. I can almost guarantee that once the barriers are found, some in the organization will not want the barrier removed.

Assume students are being interviewed regarding why some students drop out of high school. Students point to the discipline policy. They say it is not fair for a student who misbehaves in one class period to be suspended from the whole next day. The student is now behind in six classes, not just the one where the inappropriate behavior occurred. They suggest period suspension. Do not think, however, that all faculty will approve removing this barrier. All barriers to improvement have friends. It is very easy to request that our bosses remove our barriers and be resistant to removing student barriers. Educators must not be about pushing growth but about "removing the factors limiting growth."[30]

Barrier removal must become formal; it is on purpose that leaders of classrooms, leaders of schools, and leaders of school systems remove barriers as a regular aspect of their jobs. For example, John Conyers, former superintendent in Palatine, Illinois, removed many barriers.[31] He asked his teachers to write down every district office mandate. These requirements were complied into one big list. Then the district office staff was asked to check off which mandates they personally required. Many of the items that came from teachers were not required by anybody. Therefore, Conyers sent out a note to the staffs stating which "mandates" were not required. Barriers removed.

Second, he asked his administrators who regularly had board meeting preparation duties to write down what they did and how long it took them. The finance office used these time sheets to calculate the cost of a board meeting. When the board saw this they said, "We do not want to spend our money this way," and cut the board meetings in half.

The net result of this barrier removal will be increased student and staff motivation. "Parents, politicians, and school administrators all want students to be creative problem-solvers and to learn material at a deep, conceptual level. But in their eagerness to achieve these ends, they pressure teachers to produce. The paradox is that the more they do that, the more controlling the teachers become, which, as we have seen so many times, undermines intrinsic motivation, creativity, and conceptual understanding in the students."[32]

Removing waste is analogous to removing barriers. What is wasting time and money? Toyota has made a list of wasteful practices. It would be wise for school systems to look over the list and revise for education. Their list is (1) overproduction, (2) waiting, (3) unnecessary movement of materials, (4) incorrect processing, (5) excess inventory, (6) unnecessary movement, (7) defects, and (8) unused employee creativity.[33] Toyota believes in making wasteful practices publicly visible so that all can learn from improvements.

When working on removing barriers or waste, it is so important to dig down to the root cause of the barrier or waste. This is done by asking why over and over until the root cause is located. "Most problems do not call for complex statistical analysis, but instead require painstaking, detailed problem solving. This requires a level of detailed thinking and analysis that is all too absent from most companies."[34]

School leaders who can answer yes to question 3 believe that the system is the problem and disavow force, intimidation, manipulation, and incentives, plus they continually remove barriers. If the problems are caused by the system and not the people, then the first four methods of wielding influence are unnecessary and there must be barriers that are keeping these great people from achieving their utmost success.

Vision, Purpose, Core Values, and Beliefs Question 4

Question 4 is, "Do all employees believe their job contributes to the district aim and believe their contribution is valued by their bosses?" In most organizations, "people have lost hope of ever understanding the relationship of their work to the work of others."[35] Question 4 is designed to assist leaders in creating a finely tuned organization. Dr. Deming pointed out that if the best parts were taken from the best cars by the best automobile experts, all of these parts from different cars could not be put together to make a car that worked.[36] Creating an organization that works is vastly different from attempting to manage a collection of parts.

The fishbone is a tool that graphically displays the aim of the district or division and allows everybody within the organization to see how he or she contributes to the aim of the district. Figure 1.1 is a fishbone diagram;[37] the head is for the aim and the main bones are key areas of responsibility. The sub-bones are for smaller units and even employee names. In order to answer yes to question 4, all employees must be able to find themselves on the fishbone and be able to explain how their responsibility contributes to the district aim. Further, the employees must know that their bosses value their contribution to the aim. This fishbone is in stark contrast to the traditional organizational pyramid that

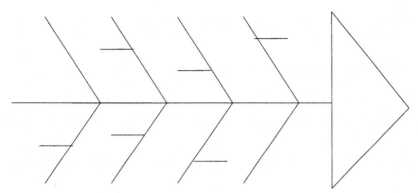

Figure 1.1. Fishbone

"only shows the chain of command and accountability. A pyramid does not describe the system of production. It does not tell anybody how his work fits into the work of other people."[38]

The aim of the school system can vary from place to place, but it always focuses upon student success. The employees in the many support units must know how they contribute to student success even though they may not even see students. Payroll is an example. How much student learning takes place the day the teacher receives a check that is short by $1,000? Not much. Many of the support staff are directly involved in student safety. They are outside the buildings and notice things that teachers inside the buildings cannot notice. They work to prevent fires, vandalism, thefts, and even intruders. No one needs convincing that fearful students cannot learn as well as comfortable, safe students. A stolen computer harms learning. Dollars spent on vandalism subtract from the musical instrument budget. It is not difficult for district leaders to directly link everyone's job to student success, but this linkage cannot be taken for granted.

Sometime it is easier for people in one profession to more clearly see their issues and problems when reading about a problem in a different industry. The defensiveness is gone because this is about somebody else, and yet the story can help educators see their own system. Deming tells of an engineer for an auto manufacturer who proposed a way to save $50 per vehicle. The current cost of electrical parts for an engine was $100 and the electrical parts for the transmission were $80, for a total of $180 for electrical parts. The proposal was to spend $130 for electrical parts on the engine and $0 on the transmission. Unfortunately, the engineer worked for the engine division and his boss said no to the suggestion. Why? The head of engines was paid a bonus on the success of engines, not cars. Thus, this $30 per engine increase would kill the annual bonus and maybe result in a pay cut.[39]

I know that there is much more to vision, purposes, and core values in education than I have written. The purpose of this book is not to rehash all that has been written but to focus only upon those beliefs that connect to systems thinking. Those who desire to have a great school system must know that the preponderance of their problems are caused by the system, that beating up on people does not fix the system, and that system barriers must be removed, and then the leaders are ready to have a system in which people are all working toward a common aim.

NOTES

1. Peter Senge, *The Fifth Discipline* (New York: Currency/Doubleday, 1990), 225.
2. Deming, *The New Economics*, 33.
3. Deming, *The New Economics*, 34.
4. W. Edwards Deming, address (American Association of School Administrators, Washington, D.C., January 1992).
5. Senge, 57.
6. Senge, 160.
7. Deming, *The New Economics*, 17.
8. Jenkins, *Permission to Forget*.
9. John C. Maxwell, *The Maxwell Leadership Bible* (Nashville, TN: Thomas Nelson Publishers, 2002), 30.
10. Deming, *The New Economics*, xv.
11. Deming, 49.
12. Maxwell, 30.
13. Deming, *The New Economics*, 28.
14. Mike Huckabee, *From Hope to Higher Ground* (New York: Warner Books, 2007), 34.
15. Deming, *The New Economics*, 43.

16. Liker, 203.

17. Kristin Meterstrom, "New York City Educator Pushes Incentives for Teachers," *Arkansas Democrat-Gazette* (May 15, 2007).

18. Senge, 340.

19. Jim Collins, *Good to Great* (New York: HarperCollins, 2001), 49.

20. Collins, 50.

21. Deming, *The New Economics*, 125.

22. Deci and Flaste, 9.

23. Deci and Flaste, 51.

24. Deci and Flaste, 51.

25. Jenkins, *Improving Student Learning.*

26. Deming, *The New Economics*, 111.

27. Deming, *The New Economics*, 113.

28. Senge, 225.

29. Deci and Flaste, 156.

30. Senge, 95.

31. John Conyers, "Charting Your Course: Lessons Learned During the Journey Toward Performance Excellence" (paper presented at the American Society for Quality's Leadership Institute, St. Petersburg, Florida, June 2004).

32. Deci and Flaste, 158.

33. Liker, 28–29.

34. Liker, 253.

35. Deming, *The New Economics*, 29.

36. Deming, American Association of School Administrators Conference, Washington, D.C. (January, 1992).

37. Michael Brassard and Diane Ritter, *The Memory Jogger for Education* (Methuen, MA: Goal/QPC, 1992), 24.

38. Deming, *The New Economics*, 60.

39. Deming, *The New Economics*, 67–68.

CONSTANCY OF PURPOSE

In order for the school board to be successful, the superintendent must be successful. In order for the school superintendent to be successful, the district must be relentless about its purpose. It must be a constant year after year after year.

Deming provided us with four generations of management, from least effective to most effective. They apply equally to the teacher leading a classroom, a principal leading a school, and a superintendent leading a school district. They are

1. *I'll just do it myself.* There is no time to teach anybody else how to do this. Besides, it probably won't be done as well as I can do it.
2. *Do it the way I tell you.* I've worked at this a long time, I'm in charge, and this is the way to accomplish the task. "Control is an easy answer. It assumes that the promise of reward and threat of punishment will make the offenders comply. And it sounds tough, so it feels reassuring to people who believe things have gone awry but have neither the time or energy to think about the problems, let alone do something about them."[1]
3. *Management by objectives*, or for children, *individualization*. MBO is written into most, if not all, state laws, as if it were the

ultimate. Educators meet with their supervisor in September to establish annual goals and then again in May to see if they were accomplished. The process is almost identical for students in that each student has his/her own goals, activities, and expectations.

4. *Agree upon an aim and work together to accomplish it.* Dr. Deming's fourth generation of management is to create a team working together toward a common goal.

Constancy of Purpose Question 1

Therefore, question 1 for constancy of purpose is, "Is there an agreed-upon aim for the work of the school district, as a whole, and an aim for every subject and operation?"[2] The aim is not the same as the mission; it has fewer words and does not describe how the aim will be met. For example, the aim could be as simple as "Increase success; decrease failure" or "Maintain enthusiasm while increasing learning." The mission statement often includes the aim but also states key beliefs regarding how the mission will be accomplished. People usually cannot remember the mission statement but can state the aim at any time.

When superintendents propose creating a district aim, staffs will naturally believe it is a waste of time. Administrivia. So here is the argument why the aim is so important. The number one complaint I hear from teachers is lack of time. Why is time wasted so often? One key reason for the waste of time is not having a common aim. When a committee is brought together to make a decision and members of the committee have different aims in their heads, a lot of time is wasted. The district aim is not imposed verbiage from the superintendent and board, but an agreement with staffs. This takes time but saves considerable effort in the future.

Maybe even more important than the aim for the district is the aim for each subject and each department. What is the aim of K–12 math, K–12 language arts, K–12 science, K–12 history/social science, K–12 arts, K–12 career-tech, K–12 physical education and health? What is the aim of district operations, finance, personnel? These agreements assist greatly in later decisions and discussions.

When teachers agree on the purpose of reading so much literature, it clearly makes novel selection easier. When teachers agree on
the aim of mathematics, it saves time in selecting activities, printed
materials, and manipulatives. It even assists in grading practices.

I suggest that the fishbone described in chapter 1 be revised for
each department and academic subject. The fish head lists the aim
for history/social science, for example. One possible aim for history/
social science is "for students to learn that people who lived before
us and people who live in other places are much more like us than
different from us." I am not recommending this aim, but can say that
up to this time it is the best I have heard. Whatever aim is chosen, it
is placed in the fish head, and the bones are the subjects within his-
tory/social science. The sub-bones are then the categories within
each division of the major categories. This fishbone for each department and academic subject communicates that the respective staffs
have agreed upon the aim of their job. They are now to do their best
to work as a team to accomplish the aim.

"A system is a network of interdependent components that work
together to accomplish the aim of the system. A system must have an
aim. Without an aim, there is no system. The aim of the system must
be clear to everyone in the system."[3] This book's twelve chapters describe improvement steps for the network of interdependent components that must work together in all school districts. Gary Convis,
writing the foreword for *The Toyota Way*, stated, "I believe management has no more critical role than to motivate and engage large
numbers of people to work together toward a common goal."[4] Establishing and living by the aim is crucial to what Gary has written.
Also, I have written about the aim for each academic discipline: Each
school subject has multiple components that must work together to
accomplish the aim of the subject. Further, "A system must be managed. It will not manage itself."[5]

Rudolph Giuliani writes, "I insisted that everyone on my staff
should concentrate on the core purpose of whichever agency or division we oversaw."[6] Readers who have read his book know that
many agencies in New York City did not know, or agree upon, their
core purpose. The police department tracking time to respond, and

not crime reduction, is a story well-told by Giuliani. Likewise, in education there is often not agreement upon the core purpose. This must not be.

When these documents are in place, the district is ready for question 2: Are students and employees given freedom to explore alternative ways to accomplish the aim of the system and the aim of particular subjects and operations? I am arguing for flexibility within an agreed-upon structure. Russell Ackoff describes the structure this way: "strategic decisions are centralized and tactical decisions are decentralized."[7] "Cap-Stat's (police records) emphasis on numbers gives some critics the impression that it is a coldly analytical way to go about achieving a goal. In fact, the opposite is true. By emphasizing results rather than methods, commissioners hold their managers responsible for improvements on their performance indicators but also give them considerable latitude to experiment with achieving those improvements."[8]

For example, during my California public school career, teachers were forced to change from using phonics to using literature as the foundation for beginning reading instruction. A few years later, these same teachers were forced to change from literature to phonics. Both decisions were wrong. The aim of reading instruction is to develop students who can and do read. Teachers who preferred phonics were forced to use children's literature, and teachers who were very successful with children's literature were forced to use phonics. This should not have occurred.

If an aim for reading had been agreed upon in California and if successful teachers had been left alone, millions of teacher hours could have been saved. But if there is no aim, chaos ensues. Deci, reporting on research findings, writes, "People who were asked to do a particular task but allowed the freedom of having some say in how to do it were more fully engaged by the activity—they enjoyed it more—than people who were not treated as unique individuals."[9] Both educational institutions and businesses need innovation and innovative people. It is the common aim and the decision of leadership to allow people freedom to find alternative methods that fuel innovation. The eighth-grade social studies teacher who insists on spending the majority of the year reteaching fifth-grade social studies instead of eighth-grade curriculum must be stopped. Freedom is being abused in this situation. However, the teacher who has creative methods for teaching district curriculum and evidence of success should not be hampered. "In fact, an integral part of successful standards implementation is greater flexibility for the teacher."[10] "*BusinessWeek*'s list of the World's Most Innovative Companies recognizes that developing breakthrough products, revamping operational processes, and coming up with new business models doesn't happen overnight. Instead of relying on gimmicks . . . they're working to build organizations that are capable of sustained innovation."[11]

We are currently misusing research to force our wills on others. Assume research proves that a particular teaching strategy is successful only 10 percent of the time. Further assume a teacher within your school district has used that strategy for years. What now? It is reasonable to present the research to the teacher and then study learning results together. If the teacher is one of the 10 percent who are successful with this particular approach, do not force a change. Leave well enough alone.

The same management style that many teachers abhor in their administrators is practiced by these same teachers. The students have no flexibility and must deliver the assignments precisely as told. When the aim is clear, it should not matter how the student demonstrates learning.

Appendix A is a student interdisciplinary assignment form from an Arizona high school. The concept is for students to request permission to create a unique paper or project that encompasses the learning requirements from two or three teachers. Students describe their proposal, write down the learning criteria for each involved teacher, and then obtain two or three teacher signatures along with one due date for all teachers. Students may spend two hours following teacher number one's direction and a couple more for teacher number two. However, when students can add their own interest, they can literally spend 100 hours on the project. Creativity will ensue, which "involves decisions that were not expected."[12] I encourage middle-school and high-school faculties everywhere to agree upon such a form and include it in their student handbook.

Ackoff supports such a practice with his provocative writing. "One of the greatest disservices of formal education lies in the fact that students are made to believe—because of the way courses and curricula are organized—that every problem can be placed in a disciplinary category, such as physical, chemical, biological, psychological, sociological, political, ethical, and so on. However, there is no such thing as a disciplinary problem."[13]

Constancy of Purpose Question 2

Common aim and individual talents are twins. Without the common aim, individual talents result in a very disjointed school system. Everybody doing his or her best in an uncoordinated fashion creates frustration. Likewise, a common aim in the hands of a dictator who does not respect individual talents and personalities creates regimentation and much unhappiness. Out of the minds of these despots come scripted lessons, daily imposed pacing, and Title I money used to hire "coaches" whose real job description is to spy and inspect.

If a school district staff, board, and citizens agree that one component of a successful language arts program is editing, then the following process might occur. First, the staff must agree upon the errors first graders are to find, then the additional errors in second grade up to middle school. At the same time, the senior English teachers are agreeing on all the errors graduates are to edit, then subtracting some for eleventh grade and so on until the two alignment trains meet in the middle. Because of differences, the teachers will then need to agree upon changes to achieve a coordinated list of editing expectations. Educators often ask which is best, starting at high school and working backwards or starting at first grade (or kindergarten) and working up. The answer is both. It seems that starting with high-school seniors and working backwards would be the ideal. The problem is the high school might not be expecting enough. When the alignment train starts in first grade or kindergarten, the expectations could be raised for seniors. So where to start is not an either-or, but both.

Now comes the point of question 2 under constancy of purpose. Are teachers and schools free to use this guideline to create the expected editors utilizing their own interests, interests of students, and their talents? Can a teacher make up an editing exercise with a paragraph about trucks because a few students are very interested in trucks? Or is there a dictator hired to write the 180 daily editing practices and then inspect teachers to be sure they complete this editing by 9:15 a.m. each day?

Lloyd Sieden, writing about the life of Buckminster Fuller, states Bucky's thoughts: "Educators with the most honorable intentions, stifle rather than stimulate children's minds, just as their own minds and creative thinking processes were obstructed by the dogma of former generations."[14] Unless leaders take a proactive stance on flexibility and creativity, within the parameters of a clear aim, 100 years from now yet another author will quote a twenty-first century Bucky Fuller with the same exact thought.

Two of Senge's points can summarize the first two questions of this chapter. "The combination of mission, vision and values creates the common identity that can connect thousands of people within a large organization." This statement is the essence of question 1 under constancy of purpose. Once this connection is established, we must recognize the difference between "two fundamentally different types of problems. Convergent problems have a solution: the more intelligently you study them, the more answers converge. Divergent problems have no correct solution. The more they are studied by people with knowledge and intelligence the more they come up with answers which contradict one another. The difficulty lies not with the experts, but in the nature of the problem itself . . . an example of a divergent problem is, 'How do you most effectively educate children?' Different people of integrity and intellect will, inevitably, come to very different conclusions."[15] This is the essence of question 2 under constancy of purpose.

In order to answer yes to question 2, teachers, principals, and even students must know the method is not the issue, but the results are what it is all about. We need no longer swing from complete individual autonomy to dictators and back to autonomy. With a common aim in place and agreed-upon expectations, much freedom can be given for people to bring their talents and personalities into play.

Starbucks has the same issue, and they only serve coffee. They want people all over the world to have a common experience when they walk into a Starbucks and yet allow the individual employees to use their own personalities. If this can be accomplished for something as small as a cup of coffee, certainly school leaders can bring about the same result for their school systems.[16]

One other impact of the common aim and constancy of purpose is to avoid the perennial debates between process and content. Michael Thompson eloquently writes, "We need not be lured into a specious choice between excellent content and excellent process ('I do not have time for thinking skills, I have to cover the material!' or 'We do not need to read books, we're training these brains to think for themselves!'): it is a false dichotomy. There is no need to choose between process and content: as teachers, we always have the exciting opportunity to apply higher-level thinking processes to higher-level content."[17]

Constancy of Purpose Question 3

Question 3 under constancy of purpose is designed to assist the school district with technology decisions and assure itself that technology is assisting the district in meeting its overall aim and each department in meeting its aim. The question is, "Is there evidence that innovation (including technological innovation) solves problems and helps various divisions meet their aim?" The key points of question 3 could have been included under question 2. However, I chose to separate technology because of the huge impact modern technology is having upon education and the whole world.

Deming referenced an advertisement for technology. "Computerized quality information systems provide the vital link between high technology and effective decision making." He then wrote, "I wish management were as simple as that."[18]

Not all technology is an improvement. My father tells me that, in his opinion, the worst invention during his lifetime was the cigarette-rolling machine. During his youth, people rolled their own cigarettes and the result was a crumpled, nonglamorous cigarette. Then along came this new technology that rolled cigarettes. Manufacturers could now advertise cigarettes as being glamorous as well as manly. The population of potential tobacco customers doubled, and thousands of women died of tobacco-related illnesses.

I would never say that educational technology has the potential for such harm, but not all educational software is helpful. "A long-awaited federal study of reading and math software that was released last week found no significant differences in standardized-test scores between students who used the technology and those who used other methods."[19] *The New York Times* reported that laptops were not helping in Liverpool. "'After seven years, there was literally no evidence it had any impact on student achievement—none,' said Mark Lawson, the school board president here in Liverpool, one of the first districts in New York State to experiment with putting technology directly into students' hands. 'The teachers were telling us when there's a one-to-one relationship between the student and the laptop, the box gets in the way. It's a distraction to the educational process.' Liverpool's turnabout comes as more and more school districts nationwide continue to bring laptops into the classroom. Federal education officials do not keep track of how many schools have such programs, but two educational consultants, Hayes Connection and the Greaves Group, conducted a study of the nation's 2,500 largest school districts last year and found that a quarter of the 1,000 respondents already had one-to-one computing, and fully half expected to by 2011."[20]

Deming wrote about his business experience, "If the reader could follow me around in my consultations, he would perceive that much automation and much new machinery is a source of poor quality and high cost, helping put us out of business."[21] Maybe when assessing the effectiveness of software programs we need pretest information on student attitudes toward school and particular subjects as well as pretest information on academic knowledge. In order for particular technology to be deemed successful, it must show increases in enthusiasm as well as academics.

So to answer yes to question 3, school districts must have evidence that technology expenditures are solving problems. For example, administrators providing a smart phone loaded with a photo of each student clearly show an improvement in questioning students about an incident or potential problem.

Some technological expenditure has become as necessary as plumbing, heating, or electricity. The servers, routers, e-mail systems, and a fully functioning computer for each teacher, administrator, and most other staff members are essential in today's world. Beyond these basics, we owe it to ourselves to be sure the technology is bringing the desired results. In chapter 10 is a description of the correlation chart. School systems should correlate the results from the educational software and the results from the state academic assessments.

My purpose in writing this portion of chapter 2 is to assist leaders as they corral technology to meet the aim of the district and aim of each department and academic subject. A quote from Sir James Dyson can summarize the power of question 3, "My business plan is to use technology to create a better product that solves a problem and is well designed. Do that and people will want to buy it."[22]

Collins writes, "Technology and technology-driven change has virtually nothing to do with igniting a transformation from good to great. Technology can accelerate a transformation, but technology cannot cause a transformation."[23]

School system leaders might do well to establish technology principles absent of discussion about any particular product. Toyota's principles can assist leaders in this dialogue. They are

1. Use technologies to support people, not to replace people. Often it is better to work out a process manually before adding technology.
2. New technology is often unreliable and difficult to standardize. A proven process that works generally takes precedence over new and untested technology.
3. Conduct actual tests before adopting new technology.
4. Reject or modify technology that conflicts with your culture or that might disrupt stability.

5. Nevertheless, encourage your people to consider new technologies when looking into new approaches to work.[24]

Further insights from Toyota: It is so important to immediately detect quality problems. It is so important to "teach your employees the importance of bringing problems to the surface so they can be quickly solved. Unless you have a problem-solving process already in place and people following it, there's no point in spending money on fancy technology. Americans tend to think that buying expensive new technology is a good way to solve problems. Toyota prefers to first use people and processes to solve problems, then supplement and support its people with technology."[25]

"When it has accomplished as much improvement as possible with the present process, Toyota will ask again if it can make any additional improvements by adding new technology. If it is determined that the new technology can add value to the process, the technology is then carefully analyzed to see if it conflicts with Toyota's philosophies and principles . . . The important principle is to find ways to support the actual work process while not distracting people from the value-added work."[26] Remember that the best option is often "the low-tech solution."[27]

I conclude these Toyota insights with their feeling about technology departments. They "refuse to allow an information technology department or advanced manufacturing technology department to push technology onto departments that do the value-added work of designing and building cars. Any information technology must meet the acid test of supporting people and processes and prove it adds value before it is implemented."[28]

Lew Rhodes, the educator who introduced me to the work of Edwards Deming, suggests that the power of technology is not so much in increasing content knowledge but in increasing relationships. Since education is such a people business, dependent upon positive relationships between students, teachers, parents, administrators, support staff, the public at large, and the legislature, the power of technology can be captured to increase these relationships. If students can observe live lessons taught in space by an astronaut, then clearly technology can foster thousands of relationships for students and staff. Students need far fewer workbooks scanned into software and far more uses of technology to communicate with people across vast distances. Further, within the school district, students are in multiple schools. Relationships often suffer because of a lack of communication.

Constancy of Purpose Question 4

Question 4 has multiple components. When problems occur, is there a definitive process that is always used to solve problems? (Not "search for new program to buy.") Are various hypotheses tested to see what might solve problems or improve situations? Are data collected on various hypotheses, so the organization has more than a collection of opinions? When a solution is found, is there a structured way to cement the new process into the organization? Can positive changes be sustained over time?

Many times when the answer to question 4 is no, it is because the organization cannot answer yes to question 1 in chapter 1. The current leadership is saying, "Those yokels who were here before me adopted the wrong program. Now here is the correct program. Use it." The problem is that most of the people who assisted the prior "yokel" are still employed in the school district and resent the attitude.

First of all, problems occur. Does the school system have a defined process for solving problems, or does it look for a quick fix? For example, the school district is not meeting its annual goals with ELL (English Language Learners). Instead of having a defined process for studying hypotheses to improve the situation, the district changes the mathematics program for all learners. Not good. The superintendent must assign somebody the responsibility of ensuring that the defined process is followed and the school system does not revert to quick fixes when the pressure is applied.

Below is an example of a defined process for solving problems, with the ELL math problem as an example. What I have written is not the only defined process available, but my hope is that this writing will cause school districts to improve upon my suggestion and create their own agreed-upon process to address problems.

Step 1. *Gather all baseline data possible* for all mathematics learning and the ELL population. This includes the five charts described in chapter 10 for all students. In addition, circle the dots of the ELL students on the correlation chart and create a separate Pareto chart for ELL students. On a separate radar chart, include vectors for ELL as well as non-ELL students. The district wants to find out (1) is improvement occurring with the ELL population (even though not as quickly as required)? and (2) are the errors of the ELL population the same as or different from other students?

Step 2. *See if the data shows improvement.* If the ELL students are making progress and scoring higher than ever before, it is crucial that the students, their parents, and their teachers know this fact. When people do not reach goals established by outside agencies, they can become very discouraged. When the scores are better than ever before, celebrate this success as a foundation for future work. On the other hand, if the results of the ELL population are stagnant or even worse, declining, this data will factor into future directions.

Step 3. *See if the subset of students is making the same errors as the remainder of the population.* Comparing the two Pareto charts (one for ELL and one for non-ELL) will provide this information, as the Pareto chart gives percentage of errors.

Step 4. *Experiment.* Require all with major responsibility for ELL students to conduct an experiment to see what will bring about improvement.

Step 5. *Study the results of the experiments.* A caution here is appropriate. If an experiment is conducted in eighth grade and the results show that this year's eighth-grade ELL students outperform last year's eighth-grade students, we do not know if the experiment caused this or the fact that there are different students. We also do not know if the teacher was so excited about the experiment that her excitement caused the improvement, and this practice probably cannot be transferred to others. Thus, the experiment should be fine-tuned for a second year. The district can find the experiments that brought about improvement in ELL math and ask teachers to experiment the next year with one of the strategies that brought about improvement.

Step 6. *Agree upon which approach(es) bring about improvement.* Once this agreement has been reached, all ELL students can then be assisted as the result of the experiments that were conducted.

Step 7. *Start over.* The school system will never be perfect, and the new Pareto charts will show errors again. They will not be the same as before the prior process, but will be errors nevertheless.

In order to answer yes to question 4, school systems need to have the agreed-upon process in place prior to big problems. Otherwise, when the pressure is present, the tendency is to make radical changes, destroy years of prior work, and change people into robots who just have a job to do. Toyota's process is to "succinctly state the problem, document the current situation, determine the root cause, suggest alternative solutions, suggest the recommended solution, and have a cost-benefit analysis." This is to be placed on one sheet of 11x17 paper with as many figures and graphics as possible.[29]

The foundation for question 4 is Deming's Plan-Do-Study-Act. Much literature has been written on the topic. This literature can assist leaders as they work to establish a culture of PDSA instead of rapid, panic-induced, quick changes.

Readers of the narrative for question 4 of this chapter soon realize that quick fixes are not recommended. Jim Collins's advice may help us. He writes, "People who say, 'Hey, but we've got constraints that prevent us from taking this longer-term approach,' should keep in mind that the good-to-great companies followed this model no matter how dire the short-term circumstances."[30] Collins also references Kroger, which "like all good-to-great companies developed its ideas by paying attention to the data right in front of it, not by following trends and fads set by others."[31] Robert Kaplan and David Norton note that an overemphasis on short-term fixes causes a problem with "the intangible and intellectual assets that generate future growth."[32]

NOTES

1. Deci and Flaste, 1–2.
2. Jenkins, Roettger, and Roettger, 5.

3. Deming, *The New Economics*, 50.

4. Liker, xii.

5. Deming, 50.

6. Rudolph W. Giuliani and Ken Kurson, *Leadership* (New York: Hyperion, 2002), 174–75.

7. Ackoff, 30.

8. Giuliani, 90.

9. Deci and Flaste, 34.

10. Douglas B. Reeves, *The Leader's Guide to Standards* (San Francisco: John Wiley and Sons, 2002), 66.

11. Jena McGregor, "Most Innovative Companies," *BusinessWeek* (May 14, 2007): 52–54.

12. Ackoff, 28.

13. Ackoff, 207–28.

14. Lloyd Steven Sieden, *Buckminster Fuller's Universe* (Cambridge, MA: Perseus Publishing, 1989), 29.

15. Senge, 284.

16. Joseph A. Michelli, *The Starbucks Experience* (New York: McGraw-Hill, 2007), 20.

17. Michael Clay Thompson, *Classics in the Classroom* (Unionville, NY: Royal Fireworks Press, 1995), 48.

18. Deming, *The New Economics*, 17.

19. Andrew Trotter, "Major Study on Software Stirs Debate," *Education Week*, (April 11, 2007): 1.

20. Andrew Trotter, "Seeing No Progress, Some Schools Drop Laptops," *New York Times* (May 4, 2007).

21. Deming, *The New Economics*, 15.

22. Chuck Salter, "Failure Doesn't Suck" (interview with Sir James Dyson), *Fast Company* (May 2007): 44.

23. Collins, 11.

24. Liker, 39.

25. Liker, 138.

26. Liker, 160.

27. Liker, 164.

28. Liker, 168.

29. Liker, 157.

30. Collins, 172.

31. Collins, 69.

32. Robert S. Kaplan and David P. Norton, *The Balanced Scorecard* (Boston, MA: Harvard Business School Press, 1996), 22.

II

THE PEOPLE

3

DEVELOPMENT OF PEOPLE

In order for the school board to be successful, the superintendent must be successful. In order for the school superintendent to be successful, the district must have success in continually developing its people.

Development of People Question 1

Has the school district calculated the average investment in each employee's personal development over the course of his or her career? in each board member over his or her tenure?

Calculating costs may seem like a very strange place to start, but it is the reality of dollars invested that causes people to further ponder their situation. "Data is valuable because it represents important information about your processes . . . Data also can surprise you or clarify a situation that was previously unclear."[1] When leaders learn they are investing over $100,000 in the staff development of each teacher, they immediately wonder if they are getting their money's worth. What kind of school system are we creating for this large investment? Remember, "Problems are not out there waiting to be taken, like apples off of a tree. They are abstractions extracted from reality by analysis."[2] I want school leaders to truly analyze the whole of their staff development investment.

The steps for calculating the investment in each teacher's staff development are

1. Calculate the amount of money each teacher earns due to column changes over the course of their career. The decision to pay teachers for almost any course they choose to take is the largest staff development expenditure in most school districts.
2. Calculate the total cost for teachers attending conferences, including the cost for substitutes. Divide by the number of teachers to obtain an average cost per teacher per year.
3. Calculate the total cost of district-provided inservice. Divide by the number of teachers to obtain the average cost per teacher.
4. Calculate the total cost of employees whose job is staff development. If an employee is 50 percent staff development and 50 percent other duties, prorate the expense. Divide by number of teachers.
5. Calculate the average number of years teachers are employed in your district. Add up costs for two, three, and four above and multiply by the average number of years teachers are employed in the district.
6. Add together the total average investment in each teacher's staff development by adding up one and five. This number will probably exceed $100,000.
7. Calculate the investment in staff development for board members, administrators, and support staff. Typically, this will be easier for these groups as there are usually no column changes for taking college courses. However, if bonuses are awarded for advanced degrees, this cost must be captured.

Once the total staff development investment is calculated for each category of employees and the board, the table is set for serious discussion about the effectiveness of processes and programs for the development of people. When leaders see that over $100,000 is invested in the development of each teacher over the course of his or her career, thinking about the issue moves into high gear. In a Pennsylvania school leadership study of educators with administrative credentials, many admitted they had an administrative credential because it was easy to obtain a master's degree this way. Think about it—the school system is paying teachers thousands of dollars for a master's degree they never intend to use.[3]

A couple of other points on the calculations are important. When administrators attend staff development during a portion of their contract, their daily rate should be charged to staff development. When any staff member goes to a seminar on new laws or other management changes, this event probably should not be charged to staff development. These annual meetings are not developing people (the purpose of staff development); they are just a part of the job. I would also argue that the meeting with the sales representative to assist teachers with the new textbook series is not staff development; it may save time learning about the resources in the new materials, but rarely do these meetings develop our teachers into better educators.

Readers can see that value judgments are included in the calculations, but these numbers are the foundation for deep discussion about how to develop the full potential of employees, board members, and students.

Deming wrote, "The benefit of training can not be measured. The cost we know; it shows on the ledger, but the benefits, no."[4] The staff development program can be managed, even though the benefits cannot be measured. "It is wrong to suppose that if you can't measure it, you can't manage it—a costly myth."[5] I assume it is true for business that the costs for training are known, but it is not true for education. The costs for the staff development coordinator, the costs for any other curriculum specialists, and the costs for conferences are known. However, the biggest staff development program is located in the personnel office and does not appear on the ledger. This staff development program is "take any university course you desire and we'll pay you $100,000" over the course of your career.

Readers must not infer that this section is a criticism of university professors. It is a criticism of the staff development process. Should school systems determine that they needed an organized, versus random, staff development program, many university professors would be invited to teach selected content.

Development of People Question 2

Question 2 asks, "Is there a structure in place for the development of teachers, administrators, support staff, students, and board members?" "There is nothing more important to an individual committed to his or her own growth than a supportive environment."[6]

Basic to building this plan is the understanding that a significant portion of the strategy has nothing to do with specific job responsibilities. All of the employees, board members, and students can grow in these foundational aspects of their lives. "One of the most dramatic changes in management thinking during the past fifteen years has been the shift in the role of organizational employees. In fact, nothing better exemplifies the revolutionary transformation from industrial age thinking to information age thinking than the new management philosophy of how employees contribute to the organization."[7]

Here I am relying upon the expertise of Dr. Vic Cottrell, president of Ventures for Excellence. He has described in great detail the qualities of excellent employees, board members, and students.

To illustrate the common desired attributes I am listing side-by-side language from Cottrell.

Board Member: Manifests a primary motive to be of service to people.

Superintendent: This person is highly committed to serving and mobilizing students, parents, board members, teachers, administrators, and other community people.

Administrator: This person believes the very best use of time is providing learning and growth opportunities for others.

Teacher: Student growth and development is seen by this teacher as the most important reason for teaching.

Support Staff: A great deal of satisfaction is derived from being supportive of the successes of others.

Student: Realizes that anything chosen to do in life needs to benefit people and society.

I recommend that readers of this book immediately request from Ventures for Excellence (www.venturesforexcellence.com) "Qualities of Excellent Employees, Board Members, and Students." It will be immediately apparent that at least half of the attributes are not job-specific. Yes, there are slight differences, but as you can see under the heading "Mission of Service," the descriptors are very similar. Cottrell's qualities are divided into "Sense of Purpose" ("Mission of Service" is a subset of "Sense of Purpose"), "Human Interaction," and then other specific job-related qualities.

Once leaders responsible for staff development have a clear picture of their ideals, the next step is identifying group strengths and areas of concern. For example, in a study of 100 school administrators, Ventures staff found these strengths and areas of concern.

Sense of Purpose Apparent Strengths:

Express finding purpose primarily through service to people
Strive to be positive in working with employees

Sense of Purpose Areas of Concern:

Have a clearly defined process of documentation to terminate in-
effective employees
Have specific strategies to involve parents in substantial ways

Human Interaction Apparent Strengths:

Desire to have very positive relationships with students
Communicate frequently with employees on a one-to-one basis

Human Interaction Area of Concern:

Describe specific effective ways of building good relationships with employees when under criticism

Describe specific ways of facilitating ongoing effective employee communication with each other

Specific Job-Related Strengths:

Express excitement about new ideas and approaches in education and management

Express a willingness to alter poor decisions

Specific Job-Related Areas of Concern:

Consistently seek input from employees to determine their high motivation areas

Include students in the organizational planning of the school

For school districts to answer yes to question 2 under development of people, the district must agree upon desired qualities. The district can use Cottrell's list of qualities or develop its own. If Cottrell's list is used, people must read and understand the qualities before adopting them as their own.

Once the qualities have been agreed upon, the next step is to determine the strengths and areas of concern for a particular school district (or region for larger districts). The strengths and areas of concern can be determined by asking for anonymous feedback. Teachers provide feedback for administrators, students for teachers, and all for support staff, the superintendent, and the board. It will then be easy to identify collective strengths and areas of concern. Example board survey questions, which were provided by Vic Cottrell, are

The board members:

1. Maintain a commitment to provide the best education possible for students

2. Maintain a belief that progress can be made within the schools
3. Look for the best intentions of others
4. Remain positive even when working through difficult situations
5. Praise the accomplishments of other board members

Staff within the school district indicates for each statement whether it is true for

Almost no board members
Few board members
Half of the board members
Most of the board members
All or almost all of the board members

The third step necessary to answer yes to question 2 under people development is to have a plan for each group of people regarding areas of concern. When the principals, as a group, receive the collective data from all the district teachers and school support staff, their job is (1) to not be defensive and (2) to learn. The learning will come from each other, from outside consultants, and from written materials. The data can become the focus for the administrators' professional learning community. In a group of principals, most likely one of them will have a highly developed strength in an area of collective weakness. For example, maybe only one principal in ten will have strength in involving students in schoolwide planning. The other 90 percent have their in-house expert and can learn from her. When this topic is fully developed and explored, the group is ready for the next area of concern, and most likely different principals will provide the expertise. It should also be remembered that many times strength can be coupled with an area of concern so that the group can easily parlay strength into strength.

A yes answer to question 2 means that the school district has determined the qualities it desires in its employees, board members, and students; it means the district has assessed itself to determine strengths and areas of concern; and finally it has an organizational plan for helping everyone become his or her best. All districts must remember there are no perfect board members, no perfect employees, and no perfect students. Everyone can grow and develop during his or her whole life. Remember Deci's words when putting together this district structure for development of people: "The truth is that there are no techniques that will motivate people or make them autonomous. Motivation must come from within, not from techniques. It comes from their deciding they are ready to take responsibility for managing themselves."[8] The structure I have described is not a technique but a systematic process to assist people one by one. Since the purpose of schools is student learning, it is worth requoting Roland Barth. "Ultimately there are two kinds of schools: learning-enriched schools and learning-impoverished schools. I've yet to see a school where the learning curves of the youngsters are off the chart upward while the learning curves of the adults are off the chart downward . . . Teachers and students go hand in hand as learners—or they don't go at all."[9]

Development of People Question 3

Question 3 is, "Is there a structure in place for the development of leaders—teachers, administrators, support staff, students, and board members?" Districts need two types of leaders: those with positions of leadership and those leaders who remain in their current positions with no official leadership capacity. The district that can answer yes to this question has a plan for both types of leadership development.

One product that might come from groups of employees working on areas of concern/areas of strength could be a new employee handbook. Starbucks employees are "given a 104-page booklet they complete within their first 90 days of employment."[10]

One cannot have too many leaders. School districts need student leaders; support staff leaders in every category; teacher leaders at every grade level and in every academic discipline; administrator leaders in instruction, personnel, operations, and finance; and board member leaders that other board members admire and follow. Not everyone in a particular position desires to lead others, but some do have a passion for leadership and will welcome mentoring.

First of all, what structures are in place to develop leaders who wish to remain in their current positions? Is there an agreement on pay for employees to present to other employees on formal staff development days (i.e., two hours of pay for preparation time)? Are department chairs and grade-level chairpersons ever brought together for assistance with their responsibilities? Is it in the job description and on the evaluation forms that administrators must develop future leaders and assist the current leaders? Is there a system in place to remind administrators of their responsibility to show appreciation for these leaders at all levels of the organization?

When administrators are thinking about the prior paragraph, they need to ask the questions, "Are some schools always cleaner and better organized than other schools?" "Are some school secretaries always available to assist and yet meet deadlines?" "Do some teachers seem to never waste a moment—even when the recess or passing period is two minutes away?" and "Do some principals always have more time to visit classrooms?" The answer is most certainly yes to these questions. Then it is paramount that the staff development personnel capture these strengths to assist in the development of all staff. These highly talented, effective people need to become leaders. Most of them will not change positions but will have much to share to help the organization.

Leadership development that is connected to position comes next. School districts should be making personnel decisions as if all administrators will become superintendents some day. When the assistant principal candidates file through the personnel office, all should be attempting to determine if the candidate can develop into becoming our superintendent. Collins cautions all of us not to be fooled by charismatic personalities who often do not produce the long-term results that are desired.[11] Deeper analysis is needed to make this prediction.

Toyota's philosophy on leadership development is

"1. Grow leaders from within, rather than buying them from outside organizations.

2. Do not view the leader's job as simply accomplishing tasks and having good people skills. Leaders must be the role models of the company's philosophy and way of doing business.
3. A good leader must understand the daily work in great detail so he or she can be the best teacher of the company's philosophy."[12]

Future job assignments shall be coordinated to ensure all have K–12 experience. The sequence of the appointments depends upon the administrator's prior teaching experience. For example, if an educator taught elementary school, many districts would not even interview this teacher for high-school assistant principal. However, if a school district has the long-term view of leadership development, then all else being equal, the elementary teacher is ideal for high-school assistant principal. The further career path could be K–8 principal, then high-school principal, assistant superintendent, and superintendent. I give this only as an example, but people need as many K–12 experiences as possible whether or not they ever become superintendents.

I realize that there are state regulations that make this viewpoint difficult. The regulations must be changed. Some states have an elementary administrative credential and a secondary administrative credential, which makes this leadership development more difficult. Some of these states that have this barrier then have a law that one need not be an educator to be a superintendent. These states make it more difficult to develop the type of needed leadership, and then when districts are unable to overcome the state-imposed barriers, they say, "Well, you don't even need any education experience to be a superintendent."

The foundation for the leadership development process is the fact that bosses have three sources of power: "(1) Authority of office, (2) knowledge, and (3) personality."[13] A district's leadership development is to foster much knowledge growth and communicate the appropriate use of power. "A successful manager of people develops 2 and 3; he does not rely on No. 1. He has nevertheless obligation to use No. 1, as this source of power enables him to change the process—equipment, materials, methods—to bring about improvement . . . He in authority, but lacking knowledge or personality, must depend on his formal power. He unconsciously fills a void in his qualifications by making it clear to everybody that he is in position of authority. His will be done."[14]

Deming lists projects instituted by bosses in *The New Economics*. They are automation, new machinery, more computers, gadgets, hard work, best efforts, merit pay, make everybody accountable, and so on. He says each of these "ducks the responsibility of management."[15] At the heart of a leadership development program is developing people who know how to lead versus applying pressure to employees or just adding more programs.

A big hole in leadership development in the United States is preparing teachers to be chief financial officers. I do not know the roadblocks from state to state, but if a person can become CFO with no teaching background, then a teacher should be able to earn a MBA, become a principal, and then become the CFO. Developing leaders often involves lobbying to remove barriers for the benefit of the district.

Sometimes while waiting for a conference session to start, I ask those who came in early to secure a seat on the last row how teachers feel when one of their most-admired teachers decides to enter administration. They groan in pain. I then ask them how they feel working for a principal who really did not develop his or her teaching strengths. He or she was okay, but did not really understand what it took to excel. The back-row bunch tells me that is their situation right now. Then I ask about how it is to work for a principal who hated teaching, could hardly wait to leave the classroom, and continually wanted the staff to know who was in charge. I hear horror stories. I then ask them about the law in many states that allows people to become principals with no teaching experience. They really groan now. I then inform them that they have eliminated the great teachers, the average teachers, the poor teachers, and the nonteachers from becoming principals. Who do they want to lead them? At that point, I hear that they want great teachers to become principals.

I do not want to communicate that all great teachers can become equally wonderful as principals. They cannot. However, the pool from which we select our leaders should be from those who have succeeded in their primary job. All who become administrators must understand they are no longer educators of children; they are educators of adults. Their job is to help adults (teachers, bus drivers, secretaries, instructional aides, cooks, custodians, and parents) do a better job with children. Administrators are still teachers, but teachers of adults. "The single most important job a leader has is to make other people successful."[16] The worst attribute in a leader is only looking at the short-term fixes. These leaders reason, "The adverse long-term consequences of consistent failure to enhance employee, systems, and organizational capabilities will not show up in the short run, and when they do, these managers reason, it may be on somebody else's 'watch.'"[17]

One of the educational myths is that people teach until they are tired of the classroom, and then enter administration. While this may be true for some, districts that have a plan for leadership development encourage talented young people with five to ten years of teaching to enter administration as a curriculum coordinator or assistant principal. Why so soon? It is because the average career is forty years and teaching until tired of the classroom (whatever that means) does not allow time for all the K–12 experiences necessary for exceptional leadership.

A yes answer to question 3 means that the school district has plans and procedures to assist leadership development for those who remain in their current position and for those who aspire to increasing levels of responsibility. Henry Givray's distinction between CEO and leader can assist. The CEO types are aspiring to have increasing levels of responsibility, whereas many leaders are not. He writes, "The problem's roots lie in the fact that the terms 'CEO' and 'leader' have mistakenly become synonymous. Nothing could be further from the truth. CEOs are measured by quantitative results. Leaders are shaped and defined by character. CEOs are expected to boost sales, improve profit margins, and make money for shareholders. Leaders inspire and enable others to do excellent work and realize their potential. As a result they build successful, enduring organizations."[18] I am closing this leadership section with a quote from Peter

Senge. His points underline the commitment that organizations must make to long-term leadership development.

"Most of the outstanding leaders I have worked with are neither tall nor especially handsome; they are often mediocre public speakers; they do not stand out in a crowd; and they do not mesmerize an attending audience with their brilliance or eloquence. Rather, what distinguishes them is the clarity and persuasiveness of their ideas, the depth of their commitment, and their openness to continually learning more. They do not 'have the answer.' But they do instill confidence in those around them that, together, 'we can learn whatever we need to learn in order to achieve the results we truly desire.' The ability of such people to be natural leaders, as near as I can tell, is the byproduct of a lifetime of effort—effort to develop conceptual and communication skills, to reflect on personal values and to align personal behavior with values, to learn how to listen and to appreciate others and others' ideas."[19]

Development of People Question 4

Question 4 is, "Is there evidence that the school system's staff development, over the past five years, is having the desired results?"

The feedback at the end of the seminar provides about 5 percent of the input necessary for improving staff development. As a speaker, this feedback tells me if I made a written or spoken error, what concepts were the most provocative, and the least/most helpful activities. What the feedback forms cannot tell me is if the lives of children and adults improved as a result of the seminar; this data can only be gathered long after the conclusion of a speech or other consulting responsibility. A yes to question 4 evaluates whether or not anything positive really happened as a result of the district's aim of helping all staff, students, and board members reach their full potential.

The sources of data are (1) opinions of staff, students, and board; (2) administrator observations; (3) increases in graduation rates; (4) all-time bests at the end of elementary, middle, and high-school years; and (5) staff retention rates. No one indicator by itself can give a complete picture of staff, board, and student development.

The annual survey of staff opinions is to list all staff development activities over the past five years. It must be determined what, if anything, really helps staffs improve. The staff survey includes the following:

1. A listing of district-sponsored staff development offerings
2. School-sponsored offerings
3. College courses
4. Conferences attended
5. Colleagues observed
6. Professional learning community activities
7. Other activities

A note at the end might read: "Many times people's most significant learning occurs because of informal relationships with colleagues. Please list below the other events you believe have helped you the most."

The scale for the survey might have the following six choices: "did not attend/participate in any," "no improvement from this," "one or two minor changes," "made some positive impact," "significant improvement in attitude and/or performance," and "I am not the same person as a result of this inservice."

The reason for looking back five years is to assess the staff development system. If the process of agreeing on qualities of exemplary employees, collecting feedback, and using the areas of concern as a springboard for professional learning communities or staff meetings is helpful, it will appear on the feedback.

The administrators in the district need a feedback form listing all district-sponsored staff development efforts over the past five years. Each of them should record their observations for each of the listed events and activities, stating whether each had no impact, helped a few, assisted half, improved performance for the majority, or made a positive impact on the lives of over 90 percent of staff. Kaplan and Norton suggest the descriptors "Awareness (heard of it), Participation (tried it), Preferences (believe it) and Loyalty (champion it)" for leaders to determine the effect of past staff development experiences.[20]

Graduation rate is really the ultimate measure of the effectiveness of assisting staff, board members, and students. Graduation rate is the sum total of all our efforts and if we are successful, more will complete high school. These efforts can include board policies that are increasingly helpful, staff development for teachers, powerful counseling, coaches keeping tabs on at-risk students, a bus driver who monitors progress, and administrators who seriously study the impact of all their decisions.

All-time bests are really mini-graduation figures at the conclusion of elementary and middle school plus expanded data for high schools beyond the graduation rate. The responsibility of elementary schools is to send to the middle school the best-prepared students ever. In a K–5 school, it is wonderful if the third-grade test scores are the best ever, but what really matters is the preparation of the graduating fifth graders. Are they better prepared in all measures? The same is true for eighth-grade students when they finish middle school.

For high school, beyond graduation rate are all the other measures such as average score on AP exams, scholarships, participation in extracurricular activities, ACT/SAT scores, and so on. The high-school principal needs to stand before each year's graduates and state: "This is the best-prepared class ever. The data to support this claim is listed in the program and I'll highlight a few for you."

While there are factors that contribute to all-time bests beyond staff development, it would be very hard to have five years of powerful staff, board, and student development and not see an improvement in all-time bests at grades five, eight, and twelve.

Answering yes to question 4 requires a formal evaluation system of all staff development efforts for at least five years. I remember Dr. Deming relating university alumni research. Graduates who finished college at least ten years ago were asked if any professor had made a significant impact on their life. If yes, who was the professor? The university researchers were most surprised by the names of the listed faculty members. They were generally not the ones receiving the awards, honors, and promotions.

In a similar fashion, districts that dig back for five years or more to evaluate all of their staff development will be surprised at what they learn and will then be much better able to plan for the future. Staff members will need reminders of the formal learning opportunities. In addition, they need space to provide feedback regarding how they learned—informal meeting with colleagues, professional learning community, evaluation with boss, reading a book, attending a conference, and so on. "The real job involves facilitating their (the staff) doing the activities of their own volition, at their own initiative, so they will go on doing the activities freely in the future when we are no longer to prompt them."[21]

The staff developers that communicate they have the "right" way may not receive high marks now or five years later. We can learn from Freese's advice: "I believe there is no right way to sell. Conversely, it's pointless to tell someone else that their current approach to selling is wrong. Thousands of sales methods are being used at companies all over the world. Extrapolate this further, and you'll find that an infinite number of variations exist as individual salespeople apply standard methods within their own unique territories. Not surprisingly, some sales approaches are more effective than others. They yield better and more consistent results. But we have to be careful deeming any one approach to be the 'right way,' because technically, that would mean everything else is wrong. This is an inference that has unfortunately caused many sales trainers to fall on their swords."[22]

I remember a principal publicly sharing his humble pie experience. He was so proud of his teachers and their use of a particular lesson plan structure. Then he took a six-month leave on a districtwide assignment. During the leave, he returned to his school unannounced to see his friends; no evidence of the lesson plan structure was in place. This is but one example of why the evaluation of staff development must be over a five-year period. If the staff development is effective, we can find evidence of continual implementation.

In summary, the process for improving the development of people is to determine the total scope of current staff development, develop a structure for the future (staff development and leadership development), and gather feedback for future planning.

NOTES

1. Larry Webber and Michael Wallace, *Quality Control for Dummies* (Hoboken, NJ: John Wiley and Sons, 2007), 107.

2. Ackoff, 201–2.

3. Education Policy and Leadership Center K–12 School Leadership Study Group, *Strengthening School Leadership* (Harrisburg, PA: The Education Policy and Leadership Center, 2006), 3.

4. Deming, *The New Economics*, 20.

5. Deming, *The New Economics*, 35.

6. Senge, 173.

7. Kaplan and Norton, 127.

8. Deci and Flaste, 194.

9. Quoted in Richard DuFour, Rebecca DuFour, Robert Eaker, and Gayle Kaharnek, *Whatever It Takes* (Bloomington, IN: Solution Tree, 2004), 38.

10. Michelli, 34.

11. Collins, 72.

12. Liker, 39.

13. Deming, *The New Economics*, 126.

14. Deming, *The New Economics*, 126–27.

15. Deming, *The New Economics*, 14.

16. Huckabee, 182.

17. Kaplan and Norton, 126.

18. Henry R. Givray, "When CEOs Aren't Leaders," *BusinessWeek* (September 3, 2007): 102.

19. Senge, 359.

20. Kaplan and Norton, 142.

21. Deci and Flaste, 92.

22. Freese, 8.

4

COMMUNICATION

In order for the school board to be successful, the superintendent must be successful. In order for the school superintendent to be successful, the district as a whole must have well-tuned feedback systems and policies.

Questions that need to be answered "yes" under communication question 1 are:

1. Are structured listening procedures and timetables in place?
2. Are students providing their teachers with monthly feedback?
3. Are students providing annual feedback to administrators on their attitudes?
4. Is there an organized way to gather feedback from parents and other community members?

The focus/foundation for a solid communication system is listening, listening, and listening. "If you want to motivate people, then it is more important to think about what they want more than what you want."[1]

Communication Question 1

"Voices of Students on Engagement," a high-school survey of student engagement, is an excellent example of listening communication. Districts may want to pattern their ongoing listening after some of their questions. The researchers found that nearly half of the student respondents do not feel they are an important part of their high-school communities. They asked students why they go to school. "Because I want to get a degree and go to college" was answered 73 percent of the time, but only 34 percent stated they enjoy being in school. Of particular note is that 24 percent of the students who have considered dropping out of high school indicated that a reason for considering this option was that "No adults in the school care about me." I encourage readers as they build their listening system to obtain from HSSSE (High School Survey on Student Engagement) a copy of their questionnaire and accompanying report.[2]

John Conyers, former superintendent in Palatine, Illinois, required his principals to speak once a year with all neighborhood parents whose children were in private schools to determine their happiness and potential return to the school system. By listening to parents who were not in the school, administrators gained valuable input. Dr. Conyers is a leader who spoke often of market share, customer retention, customer acquisition, and customer satisfaction, as if he were in business.

We educators are tempted not to listen because everybody thinks they know how to improve schools because everybody went to school. It becomes very frustrating to have all these so-called experts giving continual advice and criticism.

The solution to this temptation is to listen more, but now in a structured manner. I remember a controversy over naming a new school. Board members were receiving irate calls over the proposed name, so the incoming principal requested input from 300 parents. Thirty disliked the proposed name. When the school board received the report, one board member said, "I think all thirty called my house." This story is an example of the difference between listening to those who approach us and structured listening to everyone. The loud voices of the thirty caused people to not want to listen, whereas structured listening contains powerful insights.

When establishing the listening processes, sometimes we have input from all in the population under study and sometimes we have a sample. The typical questionnaires to parents with a 10 percent return rate are useless, with the returns showing "only the extremes in satisfaction and vexation, and at that only from the articulate."[3] Deming further wrote, "There have been instances in our experience when a non-response rate as low as 5 percent was found later to be seriously affecting the results."[4] The alternative is to randomly select a sample of the population and call the selected families to obtain as close to 100 percent return as possible.

Maybe the most salient reason for having structured listening systems in place comes from Senge, who writes, "As managers rise to senior positions, they confront issues more complex and more diverse than their personal experience. Suddenly, they need to tap insights from other people. They need to learn."[5] In actuality, almost every position in education is a "senior" position. Teachers clearly do not have experiences similar to all of their students. And then there are the administrators who need to supervise transportation, food services, accounting, maintenance, counselors, custodial services, payroll, social workers, secretarial services, and sometimes even the in-house attorney. There is no way to know all that is necessary to lead either the diverse group of students or the diverse group of employees without listening communication developed as fine art.

Different school systems are going to have different formats, but in order to answer yes to question 1, monthly and annual structures must be in place. The very simplest listening device is the plus/delta $(+/\Delta)$. On a monthly basis, students, staff, and parents say what went well last month and what could be done to make next month better. Teachers review the student and parent plus/deltas and forward to the principal those pertaining to schoolwide issues. Staff members fill them out for school issues, and principals forward to central office staff when appropriate. Principals fill out and provide them for superintendents. This structure of proactive listening ensures that people have a chance to at least hear suggestions for improvements and to hear what people appreciated as going really well last month. In most communities the plus/delta can be sent out electronically to parents.

In Shelly Carson's California high-school history classroom I asked a student if this plus/delta was worth her time each month. The student replied, "Yes, because Mrs. Carson makes at least one change each month based upon what we say." Establishing a goal of the number of changes one can reasonably make from all the suggestions is a sensible decision. Otherwise the people filling out the suggestions will become discouraged when not all the suggestions are implemented.

Deci writes, "Autonomy support, which is the opposite of control, means being able to take the other person's perspective and work from there . . . autonomy support functions through encouragement, not pressure."[6] People cannot provide autonomy support without listening. And since this is so important, school districts cannot leave listening to chance, but listening must be built into the structure of the system. Deci related this story of how a parent could assess autonomy support from her child's teacher. As you read the story remember that listening is the foundation for the success.

> A mother who seemed genuinely convinced of the importance of supporting autonomy in the classroom (and I think at home, as well) once asked me how she would know whether her son's teacher was autonomy supportive in the classroom. I asked whether she went to parent-teacher conferences with his teacher, and she said she did. I suggested that she pay attention to how the teacher speaks about her son. Does the teacher take the son's perspective in talking about how he is doing in school? And does it all ring true in terms of what you know about your son? If so, the teacher is probably quite autonomy supportive. If the teacher is able to take the boy's perspective when talking with his mother, it is probable that the teacher would take the boy's perspective when dealing with him.[7]

The annual "happy face" survey is invaluable to school systems for listening to student attitudes.[8] Students merely check a "happy face," "sad face," or "straight face" for each of the school subjects and for school itself. The happy face percentage for each grade level is calculated. Obtaining the results immediately is a great use for scanning machines. Sometimes this data is disaggregated by gender, and sometimes by subject. In one elementary school, for example, it was found that fifth-grade students still had their kindergarten level of enthusiasm for art, physical education, and technology. Science was almost up with these three while math and social studies were at the bottom with almost no support among the students. The happy face survey is but one listening device for adults listening to students. In general, the happy face survey starts with over 90 percent happy faces in kindergarten and gradually declines to 40 percent in eighth grade. Usually the percentage of happy faces stays at 40 percent in high school. One reason it doesn't go down further is that the students who hate school the most are not there to fill out the survey. Kaplan and Norton describe how Xerox once had a near-monopoly on copy machines. Customers "were still unhappy and surly" and were very willing to switch companies when choices were available.[9] School leaders should pay close attention to a system that starts out with close to 100 percent happiness and declines to 40 percent. When these students are the parents, they may desire other choices. (I need to say here what I say in my seminars. No teachers or administrators are getting up in the morning and saying to themselves, "Who can I discourage today?" Merely by doing their best in the current system, student enthusiasm is lost.)

Another important structure for listening can be at registration. In addition to health records, special education history, address, emergency contact, and so on, why not ask incoming parents three questions?

1. What would cause you to immediately unenroll your child from this school?
2. What do you take for granted in schools?
3. What would cause you to brag about this school?

The terms Webber and Wallace use for these questions are "must haves," "performance," and "satisfiers."[10] The first question is about must haves, the second question is about expected performance, and the third question is about satisfiers.

Parents need to have an easy way to communicate. People who travel for a living, as I do, receive constant e-mails from businesses that serve the business traveler. How was our service? The ones that ask the open-ended question hear from me—both the good and the bad news. The ones with long rating scales for each question do not learn from my experiences; it takes too much time.

Bill Watkins, principal of Kodiak High School (Alaska), included these suggestions in his newsletter to parents.

THE GROWTH MODEL AND DEVELOPING POSITIVE RELATIONSHIPS WITH STUDENTS

I have never met a student who wants to be a failure or wants to have a negative relationship with the adults in their life. Instead, I have experienced just the opposite. Someone asked me the other day if I could create a list of guidelines for building positive relationships with students. I can't write a list of detailed, step by step instructions for someone to follow, but I can write down some thoughts that make common sense for building positive relationships with any person—young or old.

Rule number one—For every negative find at least 3 to 5 positives. All people make mistakes and at times all people fail to do their best. Although, they are learning from their mistakes, they don't need others to remind them of their failures. Instead, they need people to help them focus on their strengths and their successes. Too often we continue to have a very narrow focus on the mistakes that our youth have made in the past and forget to accept and acknowledge the successes they have made in more recent times.

Rule number two—Listen. People, especially adolescents, are looking for someone who will listen to their point of view. We may not always agree with the other person's point of view, but we can certainly be active listeners and give them a chance to express themselves. When people fail, they are looking for a positive person in their life who will take time to listen to them. In the case of adolescents, if they don't have a positive adult they feel comfortable speaking to, they may turn to their peers who are experiencing the same failures. Every adolescent needs at least 5 positive adults in their lives.

Rule number three—Empower others to make a difference. Everyone has something positive they can contribute to any organization. Whether it be a contribution to their family, their school, their job or their friends, people need to feel they are empowered to make a difference. Find a person's strength or gift and empower them to make a difference.

I'm sure you can buy books and videos that provide a very specific step by step list of what to do to develop positive relationships with students or people in general. I'm certainly not a psychologist and I have not done any scientific research on the rules I listed above. I do know that after twenty-eight years as an educator, the three rules have worked for me and the students I have served.

As we continue to talk about the growth model in education and making sure our students are motivated to do their best in school, we will fail if we don't develop the kind of positive relationships necessary for students to feel they are supported even when they fail.

It may be that readers will reject the suggestions I have for structured listening. That is perfectly fine as there are many, many ways to proactively listen to students, parents, and employees. The district that can answer yes to question 1 under communication, however, has structured both monthly and annual listening devices. They do not wait for the complaint to listen; listening is a normal part of the district operations. Richard DuFour tells an example of listening to high-school students regarding the hardest thing about the first day of high school. Students said it was being lost in the presence of older students, so the school scheduled a day for freshmen to come to school one day prior to the rest of the students.[11]

"Every pedagogical decision must be evaluated in terms of the effect it will have on the kids' love of the book. If this emphasis of students over books seems inconsistent with a reverence for the classics, remember that it is no favor to the classics to teach people to hate them. The road to the classics runs through the hearts of the students."[12] Michael Thompson, English teacher, wrote these comments in his book *Classics in the Classrooms*. The book is an impassioned, well-articulated plea for classics in elementary, middle, and high school, and yet he stops to say taking time to listen to the students is of paramount importance.

Senge writes, "We always see the world through our mental models and . . . the mental models are always incomplete."[13] The best teachers I have ever worked with completely understand that even children can give us a more complete picture of the world. I noticed one day that one of my all-time favorite teachers, Marion Nordberg, placed her pencil between her index finger and middle finger. This seemed strange for a teacher of primary-age children who was supposed to set an example of good penmanship, so I asked about her practice. She stated that twenty years prior, a first-grade student was writing with his pencil held between his index and middle finger. She started to explain the proper way to hold a pencil and then stopped to listen to the student's reasoning. The six-year-old said that when he held the pencil his way, the pencil wobbled less often than the way adults usually hold a pencil. He could write more neatly. So Marion, ever a teacher who listened to students, said to the student that she would try his method for two weeks to see if he was right. If not, she'd insist he hold his pencil the "proper" way. That was twenty years earlier; the student was right. This is such a simple example of how the students have truths that can make the adult mental models more complete, or in this case completely change the mental model of the correct way to hold a pencil. It all comes from an attitude of listening.

Communication Question 2

When the school district accepts the strong possibility that the report card is a major communication device, then certain questions must be answered by the staff. The next question is, "Is communication through evaluation (grades and employee appraisal) assisting the district in meeting its aim?" Are we attempting to communicate performance comparing one student to the rest of the students, are we comparing the student's work against end-of-the-year standards, or are we using grades as a form of currency?

If class ranking is the goal, clearly state this on the report card by stating the desired percentage of As, Bs, Cs, Ds and Fs. If comparison to standards is the communication goal, then parents must be informed the first week of the school year what students are to know and be able to do as a result of taking a particular course or attaining a particular grade level. Then an A on the nine weeks report card means that a student has learned 25 percent of the year's content in 25 percent of the time. If it is a currency system with the possibility of earning a passing grade without learning the content, then communicate this to parents. Make it clear that extra credit work is available for all students who do not meet learning standards.

The report card will not communicate effectively unless the purpose of the report card is spelled out in very clear language. Different teachers cannot have different purposes for the report card. It is an appropriate use of administrative power to communicate to parents which of the three report card systems is in use.

If it is agreed that the report card is a major communication device between school and home, then additional symbols are necessary. The amount of information that can be fit into a square centimeter is not sufficient. Suggested additional symbols that staff might use in place of letter grades are below. Clearly, once faculties brainstorm what would be helpful, other symbols will come to mind.

W: See attached written note.

X: We had a conference and all the information I have is already shared.

I: See attached IEP and accompanying progress notations.

N: Incomplete work. _____ weeks are available to complete _____.

G: See attached graph of weekly progress up to date of report card.

Back to question 1, "Are structured procedures and timetables in place?" Educators need to hear from parents and students whether or not the report card is assisting in meeting the district aim. If not, then adjustments are necessary.

The report card for employees may be the only communication that is read, reread, studied, and filed. It is a powerful communication device. Is the employee evaluation assisting the employees in meeting the district aim? Ask them. Questions might be

1. I have worked in the district for _____ years.
2. I have been evaluated _____ times.
3. I have kept _____ of the evaluations.
4. _____ of the evaluations have inspired me to do better work.
5. _____ of the evaluations discouraged me from even trying.
6. In general evaluations make me feel _____.

Administrators need the same flexibility in grading employees that teachers need in grading students. Options on the district's evaluation form might be

W: See attached written comment.
X: We had a meeting on _____ (date) and I shared all my insights at that time.
G: See attached graph.

In order to answer yes to question 2, districts need to document that evaluations of staff and students are assisting the district in meeting its aim, because research has found that "deadlines, imposed goals, surveillance, and evaluations were all found to undermine intrinsic motivation."[14]

Malcolm Gladwell wrote, "The hard part of communication is often figuring out how to make sure a message doesn't go in one ear and out the other. Stickiness means that a message makes an impact. You can't get it out of your head."[15] People have no problem forgetting grades and evaluations. The problem is trying to figure out how to forget the bad grade or bad evaluation. And since grades demotivate approximately 50 percent of the students, education has a problem. Students cannot get the bad grades out of their heads.

Driving from the airports of America to my next speaking engagements, I sometimes pass the time away with talk radio. On a recent trip, I heard some unknown talker railing on and on about a program where everybody wins. The preschool students were having a race, but all won. He thought this was awful. Maybe he is right. "There is a scarcity of winners in a game. Only one player can come out on top. There is no harm in a game and no sin in winning a game, as far as I know. The human race, for reasons unknown, carried the pattern of games into grades in school."[16] I urge readers to enact policies that demonstrate (1) the love of games and the desire to have as many students participate as possible, and (2) that education is not a game. In sports we desire one winner at the end of the season; in learning we desire as many winners as possible. Are report cards assisting us with the aim of having as many winners as possible?

Communication Question 3

Question 3 is, "Does the school district have an established ratio between evaluation and feedback?"

Feedback is what the customers relate, and evaluation is what the bosses state. Thus, in the classroom feedback is what the students say and data documenting if the students learned what was taught. Evaluation is what the teachers say about the students. Districts that can answer yes to question 3 have an established policy regarding the ratio of expected feedback to evaluation. I use the term *coach* when a teacher is collecting feedback and *referee* when the teacher is evaluating.

When the teachers are referees, they read every paper, assign grades, and enter them into the grade book. When teachers are coaches, they do not read every paper. They randomly select a sample of papers and conduct an item analysis of errors. The concept of not reading every paper is difficult for many to accept. The irony is that educators all over are teaching statistics and probability. Students are assessed on state exams on statistics and probability. State officials place probability and statistics into every standards document. However, the most basic concept of statistics and probability is not used in education.

Statistics basics are

1. "When you measure quality statistically, you look for variation in a measurement between what the customer asks for and what you produce."[17] In this case, the customer is society and the production is student learning.
2. "All processes have some natural variation: you use statistics to detect abnormal variation that could cause you to produce a bad product or service. You can also use statistics to avoid testing every item that you produce. By testing a sample of what you make or deliver, you can use statistics to measure its quality and find out whether it meets customer requirements."[18]

In our example of item analysis, abnormal variation is the items missed by many students and the statistics are tally marks.

Teachers then report to the students the results of the item analysis sample and reteach as appropriate. Students need to learn "the idea that you don't have to measure every item you produce to be able to judge the overall quality of your production process."[19] Deming proved in his early census work, "Sampling increased the accuracy of the results, and saved much time and money."[20] By the time the teacher takes off the coach hat and puts on the referee hat, it is hoped that most of the students will be very successful. My recommendation for the ratio of feedback to evaluation is 4:1; that is, four times the item analysis and reteaching of errors to grading every paper. This process will never end as "there will always be an area where students do 'less well'—an area that can be targeted for improvement."[21]

A secondary teacher with five periods of the same subject would say, "Kids, you know I read twenty-five papers last evening. I randomly selected five papers from each period; the errors were tabulated. We'll spend ten minutes, or more if necessary, revisiting the concepts where the most errors occurred." An elementary teacher would have the same conversation with students, but the data would come from five randomly selected papers. People will say, "But what if random selection does not work and the five worst papers or the five best papers are selected?" Yes, a person can pick up five dice in

Yahtzee and roll five numbers exactly the same the first roll. It does happen. Likewise, it will happen on rare occasions that the teacher picks at random the five best or five worst papers. However, random selection, when practiced regularly, works out and both the teacher and students will have accurate data on the classroom errors.

Sometimes teachers at the same grade level or teachers teaching the same subject in a secondary setting will give the same assignment. This increases the sample size. For example, if an elementary school has five fourth-grade teachers and five papers are randomly chosen from each classroom, the students will hear a report on the item analysis from twenty-five papers.

Many school districts have a harmful policy requiring two grades per week per subject. Unintentionally, such board policies are saying, "No time for coaching—refereeing is what is important to us." The policy should be changed to a ratio of feedback to evaluation. With such a policy change, a science teacher would conduct an item analysis on the first four lab reports and then grade the fifth one.

Guskey and Bailey support the coach/referee concept, but with different language.[22] They write, "When teachers do both checking and grading, they must serve dual roles as both advocate and judge for students . . . Most of a teacher's grading and reporting tasks are actually formative in nature; that is, they are designed to offer students prescriptive feedback on their performance. Only occasionally must teachers combine that information in order to assign a cumulative, summative grade to students' achievement and performance."

Remember, this chapter is on communication, and the number one requirement for communication is listening. If teachers and administrators do not have structures in place to force listening, it does not occur. The 4:1 ratio forces everyone to listen. Deci's research found "that when people learn with the expectation of being evaluated, they focus on memorizing facts, but they don't process the information as fully, so they don't grasp the concepts as well . . . those who learned expecting to be tested had forgotten much more . . . evidently, they memorized the material for the test, as when the test was over, they pulled the plug and let it drain out."[23] He also reported research by Kage: "the use of evaluative quizzes to motivate learning lead to lowered intrinsic motivation and to poorer performance on the final examination than did the self-monitored, nonevaluative quizzes."[24]

Districts that have formalized the 4:1 ratio between feedback and evaluation will have teachers explaining to students, "You know that we have taken four nongraded quizzes on this content. I have conducted an item analysis on some of the papers each time and re-taught troublesome concepts. You are now ready for the graded evaluation; you have learned this! I can hardly wait to grade your papers and experience the joy of having such smart students."

A similar ratio needs to be established between principal evaluation and feedback to the principal. If teachers meet twice a year in a formal evaluation setting, then teachers need eight times a year to give the principal feedback on how the school is going. Why? It may be that without the feedback the principal will be tempted to blame some teachers for a problem, when the plus/deltas can communicate the barriers to success that only the principal can remove.

"In the 1980s, companies around the world discovered that if they wanted to compete in the marketplace, they had to dramatically improve quality while reducing costs. Companies who survived accomplished this by shifting how they managed their quality processes. Instead of relying on inspection alone to identify and correct problems, they moved toward a focus on preventing problems before they occurred."[25] The coach/referee process is merely language to communicate to students and parents the process of preventing problems before grades are assigned.

We all know that in communication listening is more important that telling. We all credit the best listeners as the best communicators. However, the policies of most school districts favor telling (evaluation) versus listening (item analysis/feedback).

Finally, collective feedback time must not be overlooked. "Teachers were more likely to acknowledge the need for improvement when they jointly studied evidence of the strengths and weaknesses of their school. They were more likely to arrive at consensus on the most essential knowledge and skills students should acquire when together they analyzed and discussed state and national standards, district curriculum guides, and student achievement data."[26]

Communication Question 4

The fourth question under communication involves responsiveness expectations. "Do regular communications to students, parents, and community provide results of feedback and improvements because of the feedback?" School districts anticipate what people will want to know and place this information on websites. They send out notices in multiple languages. This is as it should be. However, the public will always judge a district's communication based upon response to their concerns. Of course, hearing what they want to hear helps people be satisfied, but everyone cannot always be pleased. We all know this. It is the responsiveness that people use to assess real communication. Time is of the essence. "For example, a company can measure the percentage of customer complaints that are solved with a single phone call. Increasing that percentage not only bumps up quality and makes for happier customers but also eliminates the waste of follow-up calls."[27]

Response time is not limited to people leaving phone messages and sending e-mails. It is also reporting out answers to the following three questions. The agreed-upon expectation among principals is how long after the monthly plus/deltas are collected should it be before staff have the aggregated data? The response message includes the plusses from last month, the suggestions for improvement, and at least one suggestion that can be implemented before the month is over.

How long after students fill out the annual happy face survey are the results distributed? How long after the teachers collect sample work do students hear about the item analysis? How long after the state assessment results are delivered to the school district are the five basic graphs, described in the "Results" chapter of this book, made available? Do parents and students receive communication from teachers' "coaching" item analysis? For example, "The third-grade teachers conducted their weekly item analysis of students' writing and found the lack of paragraphs to be the most common error."

A yes answer to all four communication questions means that the school system has formalized its commitment to proactive listening, removed barriers to effective communication (especially report cards and other forms of evaluation), established a ratio between listening (feedback) and telling (evaluation) and finally shown great respect and welcoming through quick, accurate responses.

NOTES

1. Freese, 55.
2. Ethan Yazzie-Mintz, *Voices of Students on Engagement* (Bloomington, IN: Indiana University School of Education High School Survey of Student Engagement, 2006), http://ceep.indiana.edu/hssse.
3. W. Edwards Deming, *Some Theory of Sampling* (New York: Dover Publications, 1950), 15.
4. Deming, *Some Theory of Sampling*, 13.
5. Senge, 198.
6. Deci and Flaste, 42.
7. Deci and Flaste, 143–44.
8. Jenkins, 129.
9. Kaplan and Norton, 23.
10. Webber and Wallace, 86.
11. DuFour, DuFour, Eaker, and Kaharnek, 55.
12. Thompson, 38.
13. Senge, 185.
14. Deci and Flaste, 31.
15. Malcolm Gladwell, *The Tipping Point* (New York: Little Brown and Co., 2000), 25.
16. Deming, *The New Economics*, 147.
17. Webber and Wallace, 11.
18. Webber and Wallace, 11.
19. Webber and Wallace, 131.
20. Deming, *The New Economics*, 120.
21. DuFour, DuFour, Eaker, and Kaharnek, 139.
22. Thomas R. Guskey and Jane M. Bailey, *Developing Grading and Reporting Systems for Student Learning* (Thousand Oaks, CA: Corwin Press, 2001), 31.
23. Deci and Flaste, 48.
24. Deci and Flaste, 49.
25. Webber and Wallace, 33.
26. DuFour, DuFour, Eaker, and Kaharenk, 137.
27. Del Jones, "Toyota's Success a Boost to Lean Style," *USA Today* (May 4, 2007).

5

SAFETY

In order for the school board to be successful, the superintendent has to be successful. In order for the school superintendent to be successful, the schools must be safe.

Safety Question 1

Safety question 1: Is baseline data collected on safety? Somebody in every school district must have the primary responsibility for safety. It matters not whether or not this person holds a teaching credential. This person, often because of a prior tragedy in his or her own life or the life of a close friend, wants to do everything possible to prevent harm to others. The first responsibility of this person is to make a list of ways people are physically and emotionally harmed. Sadly, the list is long. It has to include weather, fire, intruders, sexual abuse by students or employees, toxins, fighting, bullying, and verbal abuse by employees and students.

The next step in answering yes to question 1 under safety is developing a system for collecting data on a regular basis. Crucial to improving any system is knowing the starting place. Employees and students are the source of the data for the school district. The questionnaires for staff and students start off in a similar fashion. Sample questions are

1. What do you do in an earthquake?
2. What is the signal that indicates an intruder is on campus?
3. How do you inform the office of a potential intruder?
4. What is the process to follow in case of a fire?

A change in format occurs partway through the questionnaire. For students, the directions are to write on a sheet of scratch paper the initials or nicknames of ten other students. (These lists will *not* be collected.) The questionnaire directions are to answer questions about other students, not themselves. Sample questions could be

1. How many of the ten friends/acquaintances you listed drive while drunk?
2. How many of the ten friends/acquaintances you listed smoke every day?
3. How many of the ten friends/acquaintances you listed are being bullied?
4. How many of the ten friends/acquaintances you listed are joking about killing somebody?
5. How many of the ten friends/acquaintances you listed are being embarrassed by a school employee?
6. How many of the ten friends/acquaintances you listed are at risk of getting pregnant?

School districts may also ask employees questions similar to those asked students. The adults do not list ten friends but use their knowledge of all staff, including substitutes and walk-on coaches. The survey must not ask questions about people's personal lives but must be focused upon student safety. It is verbal abuse of students, not verbal abuse of family members, that is the focus. Sample questions could be

1. To the best of your knowledge are there employees verbally abusing students? If so, how many?
2. To the best of your knowledge are there employees physically abusing students? If so, how many?
3. To the best of your knowledge are there employees sexually abusing students? If so, how many?

I would suggest that the school district's attorney review these questions for two reasons. The first is to be sure that no people's rights are violated, and the second is district protection. If a serious incident occurs on campus and the victims hire an attorney to sue the district, what questions is the opposing attorney going to ask? Be prepared.

There is a second aspect to baseline data: the graphing of normal data on school discipline and other aspects where detailed data is available. I suggest using the Pareto chart for discipline. Figure 5.1 is a Pareto chart displaying categories of discipline referrals for the middle school of 400 students in Pine Island, Minnesota. The Pareto chart places the referrals in rank order from most referrals to least and then provides the cumulative percentage on a sloping line. Graphs seem to have been reinvented in the eighteenth and nineteenth centuries. The earliest known example of a graph comes from a tenth-century graph of planetary movement.[1] And yet in the twenty-first century people think their work is done when they overload people with stacks of spreadsheets. The electronic spreadsheet is an incredible invention for collecting numbers, but it is not the report!

The next baseline data to collect is the cost of vandalism. Why? Vandalism is connected to safety; it causes people to not feel safe when their environment is destroyed or full of graffiti. Another Pareto chart can be created for vandalism costs, including graffiti. One Pareto chart can track locations and another one types of vandalism.

In order to answer yes to question one under safety, school districts must have a firm, detailed grasp on current safety.

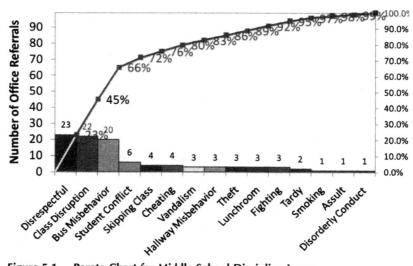

Figure 5.1. Pareto Chart for Middle School Discipline Issues

Safety Question 2

The second question under safety is, "Is the emergency preparation rehearsed on a regular basis? Is the communication system for crisis management in everyone's mind?"

The first drills that come to mind are for fire, weather emergencies, and intruders. Once these are in place and known by all, then there is the practicing of procedures for other emergencies and safety issues.

Many more students die each year from being passengers in cars driven by intoxicated drivers than are killed by intruders. What should students do when confronted with such a possible emergency? What should students do when they know bullying, verbal abuse, sexual abuse, substance abuse, and fighting are taking place? A district that can answer yes to question 2 under safety has established time lines for practicing all safety-related issues. Further, data collection, establishment of procedures, organization of drills and assemblies, organization of communication in emergencies, and coordination of improvement efforts should be housed in one office. The drug, alcohol, and tobacco abuse initiatives; the safety officers; and the emergency preparation should be coordinated as one unit totally committed to student and staff safety. One person is the go-to leader for all safety issues.

Safety Question 3

Safety question 3: Is there evidence of improved safety in all aspects of safety (physical, sexual, bullying, toxins, psychological)? This question is the reason for all of the hard work related to questions 1 and 2. Does the school district have a record, over time, showing that the schools are safer in all aspects of physical, sexual, and psychological safety?

School boards, all employees, all but the youngest of students, and all parents need reports written especially for them that show a long-term decrease in unsafe practices. The aim is not to overwhelm people with piles of numbers but to document improvement. Fewer students report being bullied; fewer fights occur; fewer students report alcohol, tobacco, and drug abuse; and there are fewer incidents of vandalism. There is evidence of fewer instances of sexual abuse and intimidation.

Many are opposed to red-ribbon week and safety assemblies. Why? Both take time from classrooms. So, since safety is so very important, all need to know that the time spent was worth it. "Is all of this work paying off?" The answer to safety question 3 either celebrates improvement or redirects the efforts of red-ribbon week and assemblies because of no improvement. Both are most helpful.

Safety Question 4

Question 4 seems almost impossible: "Is there evidence of a safer school community and evidence of less expense on safety at the same time?" In May 2007 I read an article describing how the next generation NASCAR cars will be both safer and more cost-effective.[2] We can accomplish the same in schools.

A yes answer to safety question 4 might not occur for several years. The up-front investment may delay the cost savings. For example, a high-school principal told me that the school's video cameras almost completely stopped bathroom vandalism. "How?" I asked. "You can't place cameras in the bathroom." The principal stated that some cameras are at the doorway to the bathrooms. When there is a problem with vandalism in the bathrooms, the custodian checks the condition of the bathrooms every five minutes. Thus, if vandalism does occur, the administrators can narrow the potential perpetrators down to a very few. This is an example of increased expenditures that resulted in decreased long-term expenditures.

School districts that can answer yes to safety question 4 have to not only document more safe campuses but also document less money spent on safety. Readers will see that I recommend cost per pupil for noninstructional expenses. A district that can answer yes to this question can document that less money per pupil is spent on school safety and at the same time that the campuses are safer. Question 4 is a true challenge, because the public demands safe schools but would far rather spend money on another tuba than another security officer at the football game. It is over a period of five years or so that a school district should be able to show decreases in both safety-related costs and infractions.

NOTES

1. Edward Tufte, *The Visual Display of Quantitative Information*, 2nd ed. (Cheshire, CT: Graphics Press, 2001), 28.
2. Michael A. Prospero, "NASCAR Car of Tomorrow," *Fast Company* (May 2007): 58.

6

PERSONNEL OFFICE

In order for the school board to be successful, the superintendent must be successful. In order for the school superintendent to be successful, the district must hire extremely well, retain these top employees, and replace those causing harm to students.

The personnel department is responsible for the quality of the employees. The foundation for most of a school district's success is the attitude, skills, and qualities of its employees. The superintendent and board must have a personnel leader who is totally committed to hiring and retaining exemplary employees in each and every position. The personnel director who says, "We just have a hard time filling our positions," is dooming the district for the next twenty-five years. Yes, some school districts have more applicants than positions because they are located in a university town and graduates like to stick close to their alma mater. Yes, some districts are in very rural locales and some schools serve more needy populations. Nevertheless, hiring involves decisions, and the commitment to hiring the best should be unwavering.

Jim Collins interviewed Walter Bruckart of Circuit City. When he was asked to name the top five factors that led the transition from mediocrity to excellence, Bruckart said, "One would be people. Two would be people. Three would be people. Four would be people. And five would be people. A huge part of our transition can be attributed to our discipline in picking the right people." "Bruckart then recalled a conversation with CEO Alan Wurtzel during a growth spurt at Circuit City: 'Alan, I'm really wearing down trying to find the exact right person to fill this or that position. At what point do I compromise?' Without hesitation, Alan said, 'You don't compromise. We find another way to get through until we find the right people.'"[1] "Great vision without great people is irrelevant."[2]

Personnel Question 1

Therefore, the first question to be answered in the affirmative for personnel is, "Does the district have a structured recruitment/ interview/hiring/retention process?" Does it have a way of finding people with the healthiest mental health—people who "focus on developing satisfying personal relationships, growing as individuals, and contributing to their community"?[3]

The foundation for successful personnel policies is the structured interview. Structured interviews compare the qualities of the candidate with the qualities of the most successful people in various job categories. While not all successful employees think exactly the same, when highly successful employees are interviewed, their answers are amazingly close. It is possible to compare the answers of candidates with those of exemplary employees in order to ascertain a potential colleague's success.

For example, when teacher candidates are asked how they want students to view them, responses, from worst to best, are generally (1) they want respect from students, (2) they want to be viewed as a professional, and (3) they want to be viewed as a caring, concerned, helpful person. Our best teachers know that students learn more from teachers they like. Personnel departments armed with structured interview questions along with considerable guidance in listening to the language nuances will be able to significantly increase the percentage of time schools are thrilled with new employees. Regarding nuances, for example, when questioned about the importance of writing, student teachers are allowed to state what they believe should occur. Experienced teachers are not allowed to state how it should be, but only what they did. If they did not have students write every day in their former position, they almost certainly will not if you hire them.

My experience with structured interviews comes from Ventures for Excellence in Lincoln, Nebraska. The firm, led by Dr. Vic Cottrell, has structured interviews, along with corresponding research, from great employees for every position. This firm delivers its interviews through about a dozen associates. Much of the learning process is grueling. I can remember watching countless videos of the back of Vic Cottrell's head as he faced a candidate. Vic asked a question, the candidate answered, and the recording was paused while all of us scored the candidate's answer. We had before us the responses of poor employees, average employees, and great employees and compared the video candidate's answer to the language before us. Discussion took place and then the Ventures leader provided the official scoring and rationale for the score. We experienced interviews with great, average, and poor candidates in our training.

I have related a glimpse into the training required for personnel departments to become competent in their most important job. In order for a school district to even begin to answer yes to the first question in personnel, the department must have a series of structured questions (with accompanying research from great employees) for all positions. In addition, candidates must go through a series of interviews with several highly trained people comparing notes from the structured interviews.

Vic Cottrell states over and over that while the skills of teaching can be learned on the job, selflessness and the ability to create positive relationships cannot be learned on the job. "What Meyer (restaurant owner) can't do is instill the capacity for empathy in people who don't have it. He can't make them sensitive to the way their actions affect other people. He can't give them the desire to bend over backward to ensure that customers leave feeling they've just had a spectacular dining experience because they've been 'treated to every kindness,' not just because they've received good service. And he can't teach them to care as much as he does about making sure each customer has a good time. So he hires those qualities and skills, the human skills; he trains for the others."[4]

After this series of interviews, the finalists are ready for reference calls. The district must have a series of ten or so structured questions for the reference calls. A key point in writing the questions is to not ask the former employer to evaluate the candidate. This makes them very nervous and reticent to answer truthfully. They are only to give facts, and the hiring personnel are to evaluate the answers. The personnel department of the hiring school district is listening for descriptions, not for evaluations. They want clear evidence of the attributes they are looking for in future employees. An example of a great reference question, provided by Dr. Cottrell, is, "Tell me about Joe's work habits." A poor reference question is, "How punctual has Joe been in coming to work?" Bob Poffenbarger, who used the Ventures process in his superintendency and now works with Ventures, provided his favorite reference question along with the worst reference question. Poffenbarger wrote, "How do you believe a supervisor should work with _____ in order to bring out the best in him/her?"[5] Here the reply immediately gets at problems, concerns, and areas needed for growth or quickly identifies productive behaviors for reinforcement—a great reference question.

The worst question people ask is "What can you tell me about _____ ?" This question admits the person making the contact has no clue about what they are searching for in a candidate and gives the reference opportunity (and full authority) to evade a substantive answer.

Other components of the hiring process can certainly be added—observing a teacher in action, collections of letters (often called fan mail), portfolios, and so forth. However, the foundation for selecting top-notch employees is the structured interview that compares the qualities of the candidate with the qualities of exemplary employees.

Critics of the structured interview will say, "Yes, but some people just interview better." My response is twofold. I have personally interviewed superconfident people who couldn't come close to matching the desired qualities. They communicated in the interview that they were selfish and very not at all interested in listening to anybody, and surely these teacher candidates were never going to ask students their opinions. Great interviewing skill was present, but the structured interview let us not be fooled by this display of poise. On the other hand, I have interviewed very nervous people whose red-blotched skin multiplied during the interview. The structured interview helped them share their unselfish, listening character, in spite of a lack of interviewing poise.

Secondly, the critics are partially right. When I've made a hiring mistake, even with the aid of the structured interview, relistening to the recording of the interview showed up the problem. The problem was I didn't really hear what the candidate was saying. They told me in the interview what they would be like and I didn't hear it. Occasionally, the critics are right; a candidate fools us all.

For this reason, the primary responsibility for staff development of nontenured staff rests with the personnel office. Of course, personnel is assisted by principals, instruction, and staff development, but until the probationary period is over, personnel is accountable for the success or replacement of the newly hired. The superintendent and board cannot allow the personnel department to hire and then expect the principals and various departments to deal with their poor decisions. Personnel is accountable for giving tenure, and the hiring process is not over until tenure is granted. I suggest that each year the personnel department have a place on the board agenda or time at other events for honoring newly tenured employees. All will know that tenure is not automatic.

I have found that the most difficult tenure decisions are the nonrenewals of average employees. People know that the nonrenewed probationary employee is more talented than the grumpy tenured employee down the hall. All administrators must understand that tenure is granted to great employees and not to average ones. No school district needs a bunch of average employees for the next twenty-five years. Peter Senge advises, "You must develop a strategy of aggressive hires and steadily elevating quality standards."[6] Collins writes, "The moment you feel you need to tightly manage someone, you've made a hiring mistake. The best people don't need to be managed. Guided, taught, led—yes. But not tightly managed."[7] The rest of this book is about elevating quality standards, but this section of chapter 6 is simply about hiring and retaining only the very best.

A key aspect of a personnel department's responsibility is recruitment. I remember Vic Cottrell explaining how the University of Nebraska was able to field a top-notch football team year after year. It is because coaches waited to see which high-school athletes express an interest in Nebraska and then selected from those who filled out an application. Silly.

Likewise, it is silly for personnel departments to wait for applicants. The search for top-notch employees is an everyday occurrence. Further, it must be possible for the personnel departments to hire these top-notch employees when they find them and not be constrained by a hiring calendar.

An aspect of question 1 is retaining top-notch employees. When all of this effort goes into hiring well, retention is so important. Kaplan and Norton list the six factors most important in measuring employee satisfaction. They are "involvement with decisions, recognition for doing a good job, access to sufficient information to do the job well, active encouragement to be creative and use initiative, support level from staff functions, and overall satisfaction."[8]

Personnel Question 2

Question 2 is, "Does the system have an agreed-upon process to build quality and appropriate relationships with all employees?" School districts cannot leave it to chance that employees will automatically develop positive relationships with colleagues, bosses, parents, students, and community members. It is well known that some principals have great rapport with their staffs, some teachers are adored by their students, and some support staff are able to get along with everyone. What proactive steps do they take? What attitudes do they possess? What activities do they engage in on a regular basis? The school district needs to assist people not in ways to motivate others, but in ways to "create the conditions within which others will motivate themselves."[9] We must also remember that "credibility is the prerequisite for every relationship."[10]

One of the barriers to overcome in establishing a list of regular activities and consistent attitudes is the false notion that the open-door policy is the ultimate. It is not. The open-door policy is an average practice. The worst communicators talk with their friends, average ones have an "open door," and the very best are proactive about communication. What does open door really mean? It means, "If you take the initiative to come by to see me, my door is open and you can come in. However, if you do not take the initiative we'll never talk. I'm in my office." The best communicators have practices that say, "I am going to listen to you where you work." This can mean the lunchroom where the principal is listening to students, the parking lot where the principal is listening to parents, or the school staff room where the superintendent is listening to staff. The people who are the best at communication do it mostly outside their office.

Those in the personnel office must never forget that relationships at home matter also. "One cannot build a learning organization on a foundation of broken homes and strained personal relationships."[11] When personnel officers make decisions that help out employees in a time of need, they are truly creating long-term loyalty.

I conclude this section on relationships with the mundane task of job descriptions, a job that falls within the scope of responsibility for the personnel office. "A job description must do more than prescribe motions; do this, do that, this way, that way. It must tell what the work will be used for, how the work contributes to the aim of the system."[12] When job descriptions are written in this manner, it assists people in their relationships because they have more respect for the work of others.

Personnel Question 3

Question 3 is, "Does the district have a structured process for documentation of poor performance?" Some employees are in the wrong profession. Everybody knows it. Yet, they survive year after year. Teachers complain about other poor teachers. Custodians complain about unsatisfactory employees. Principals complain about principals that are letting them down. The reason many teachers do not want to become administrators is they do not want to accept the responsibility for documenting and eventually firing unsatisfactory employees. And they know every unsatisfactory employee has some friends, and the politics are tough.

Administrators need a structured written communication system. The best I know is from Mary Jo McGrath Training Systems in Santa Barbara, California. She calls for a four-part communication system named FICA. These four letters stand for

1. Facts: background information, current facts, and relevant history;
2. Impact: implications of these facts upon students, the community, the school district, and so on;
3. Context: placing the identified facts and impacts in the context in which they arise; and
4. Action: weighing the facts, impact and context to arrive at the next appropriate action.[13]

While this question focuses upon the negative aspects of the personnel department's responsibility, it must be noted that administrators who have been through McGrath's SUCCEED staff development, such as Bob Poffenbarger of Rochester, Indiana, relate that the administrators now write many more positive notes than before. Prior to the inservice and establishment of written guidelines, some were reticent to write positive notes for fear a legal problem might arise in the future. The former, positive note would come back to hurt them. These same guidelines really do assist with positive, written communication as well as the necessary negative communication.

Further, school boards, legislators, and superintendents can make it easier for administrators to document unsatisfactory employees. Some recommendations are to cut back on the required observations and evaluations of satisfactory and exemplary employees. The treadmill of many required evaluation systems all but guarantees that the poor employees will survive. Secondly, regions can organize to assist principals and department heads. The suggestion is for an intermediate service agency, or other organization with a larger service area than most school districts, to contract with retired administrators to document poor performance. These volunteers would be paid for the required inservice by a firm such as McGrath's Training Systems and paid an agreed-upon daily rate to observe in a classroom or department. The volunteers can spend a couple of days in a location because they do not have a multitude of other responsibilities. I suggest that, if at all possible, the district contracting with the retiree should find someone who formerly had the same job as the person being observed or documented. These two recommendations might not be what a district eventually lands upon, but, simply, the process is (1) ask what the barriers are to effective/successful documentation and (2) remove the barriers.

Personnel Question 4

The fourth personnel question is, "Does the personnel office have a feedback system from employees regarding all aspects of personnel responsibilities?" The personnel department needs to know (1) if the newly hired employees are satisfactory according to colleagues, (2) why excellent employees left the district, (3) if current employees are recommending that their friends apply in this school district, and (4) if employees are aware of an employee with a personal problem who received assistance from the personnel office? If so, how pleased was the employee with the assistance?

Kaplan and Norton would have organizations evaluate employee satisfaction, employee retention, and employee productivity.[14] The first two measures come from the personnel department's initiative.

"It is a pivotal moment in the evolution of an organization when leaders take this stand . . . it means that the organization has absolutely, fully, intrinsically committed itself to the well-being of its people."[15]

The feedback system to the personnel office is basically this: How have leadership decisions proven that the school district is committed to the well-being of its employees? How could decisions be improved? Are there people working for our school district, for less money, and maybe even driving further, because they know they will be well cared for?

NOTES

1. Collins, 55.
2. Collins, 42.
3. Deci and Flaste, 129.
4. Bo Burlingham, *Small Giants* (New York: Portfolio, 2005), 73.
5. Interview with Robert Poffenbarger, October, 2007.
6. Senge, 334.
7. Collins, 56.
8. Kaplan and Norton, 130.
9. Deci and Flaste, 10.
10. Freese, 87.
11. Senge, 312.
12. Deming, *The New Economics*, 64.
13. Mary Jo McGrath, "The Case of the Messy Desk," *The School Administrator* 64, no. 6 (June 2007): 30.
14. Kaplan and Norton, 129.
15. Senge, 144.

III

THE PHYSICAL ASSETS

7

FINANCE

In order for the school board to be successful, the superintendent must be successful. In order for the school superintendent to be successful, the board and superintendent must control the budget rather than the budget controlling the board and superintendent.

Finance Question 1

The first responsibility of the finance office is to keep the doors open, the lights on, the busses running, and to meet payroll. In other words, they are to avoid the disaster caused by negative spending. When school finance experts are called in to help with a financially troubled school system, the first check they often make is to compare the number of employees listed in payroll, personnel, and finance. Question 1 in finance is, "On every day of every year, do finance, payroll, and personnel have in their databases the exact same number of employees?"

Such a requirement seems simple, but it is not. A district purchases a personnel system and at great expense in both dollars and time has it up and running. The personnel system and the payroll system and the finance system have the same operational definition of an employee, and the systems talk to each other. Then some school district somewhere in the same state is in the headlines daily because of a huge fiscal crisis. The legislature feels obligated to respond, so new, more complex software is mandated for the finance offices of all school districts in the state. The new software is installed and seems to work, but the software in finance and the software in personnel/payroll do not talk to each other. Readers can add their own horror stories as to why payroll may add yet a third software program. The table is set for disaster. Nevertheless, the problem must be solved, first by making sure all three programs have the exact same definitions of employees and then making sure the programs talk to each other. The district that can answer yes to finance question 1 can state that 365 days a year the numbers are the same.

There are other ways for school districts to enter a fiscal crisis, such as in Oklahoma, where the state legislature recently reduced the income to school districts five different times after the start of the school year. School districts do not have control over state crises, but they do have control over the answer to question 1. And since payroll accounts for 80 to 90 percent of most school district budgets, getting this number right is crucial.

Finance Question 2

The reason school districts have reserves is because nobody can guarantee that a district's budget will balance. A hurricane can hit the last day of school. However, a school district can calculate the probability of a balanced budget on a regular basis. The purpose is to have in place an early warning system. A tension exists in many school districts between the instructional side of the staff, which wants to spend this year's income on this year's students, and the financial side of the staff which wants to save as much as possible, building up the reserve. Further, because of the fear of going broke, some school board members not only want to approve the budget (their job), but they want to study each and every expenditure (not their job). To help avoid these conflicts and to assist responsible people in making prudent decisions, finance question 2 is provided. It is, "Is there a monthly budget synthesis that serves as an early warning system?" "Measurement is the compass you use on your organization's journey to quality. A proper measurement process tells you where you've been, warns you if you get off track, and lets you know when you hit your goal."[1] In school finance, school districts do have good records of where they have been and do know if they hit the goal of a balanced budget. This question deals with the middle—the warning mechanism.

Until the school year is over, all payroll and all invoices have been paid, and all income has been received, there is a chance the school district will not have a balanced budget. My advice is to prepare for school leaders and school board members a two-page summary of the school district's finances each month. One page is income, and the other is expenses. Right now, school board members are usually provided a computer printout of every fiscal transaction the past month. I suggest that this overkill is not an early warning system. Most school systems that find themselves in serious financial trouble have at least one board member who reads every monthly transaction. So, what should an early warning system look like?

School finance includes multiple assumptions on both the income and expenditure sides of the ledger. School finance runs into trouble when the assumptions are wrong. Since the budgeting process begins eight to nine months before the start of the school year, the budget must be based upon assumptions. Further, many times the new school year begins before the state legislature and governor approve the budget. Assumptions are the foundation for budgets in both business and education. "In fact, accounting and finance . . . really are as much art as science."[2]

A key responsibility of the finance office is to report to the superintendent and board each month on the accuracy of the assumptions. This document is not prepared for CPAs, but for the non-CPAs who are ultimately responsible for the overall fiscal health of the school district.

In the simplest of terms, the assumptions for income are numbered with narrative, and another list of expenditure assumptions is numbered. Each month the finance office reports on the accuracy of each of the assumptions. Comparison with prior years certainly is one basis for assumptions. A few of the income assumptions are cost-of-living increases, lottery income per student, attendance, federal increases or decreases, interest rate on cash, ending balance from current year (to determine cash for next year's interest), and many, many more. The expenditures are in many different categories, but there are a few major assumptions that affect all. Some are weather, cost of fuel, savings in salary based upon anticipated retirements, insurance rates, and so on. A major assumption is that the state will actually have the income to pay the amount per pupil in the state budget.

Question 2 can be affirmatively answered when all board members and all members of the superintendent's cabinet can understand, explain, and feel comfortable with the assumptions and their updates. Every time I read about a school district in financial trouble it is because of assumptions that did not work out. What comes to mind is a sports story in which the owner of a team made an assumption that if a championship was won, the community would flock to games and pay for the high salaries of the athletes. In business, "A profitable company charts its own course. Its managers can run it the way they wish to. When a company stops being profitable, other people begin to poke their noses into the business."[3] In education, the other noses come from the legislature, the enraged public, and the unions.

"Absent such knowledge, what happens? Simple: the people from accounting and finance control the decisions. We use the word control because when decisions are made based on numbers, and when the numbers are based on accountants' assumptions and estimates, and then the accountants and finance folks have effective control."[4]

Finance Question 3

Question 3 is, "Does one person have the overall responsibility for increasing income?" School districts do not have all the opportunities that a business has to increase income. Nevertheless, they can increase income through increased attendance, dropout prevention, grant writing, renting of space, vending, after-school paid activities, and so on. If nobody in the finance office has this responsibility, it is much less likely to occur. Finance cannot be content to merely manipulate the numbers of what comes in and what goes out. Attendance is a major source of income in many states. When working to increase attendance, Kaplan and Norton's advice is salient. They write, "In general, existing and potential customers are not homogeneous. They have different preferences and value the attributes of the product or service differently."[5] More of the same will probably not convince parents educating children elsewhere that your school district is the best choice. Leadership is required, and so is smiling. "'Did you see any differences between them and us?' 'Yes, I did,' the prospect answered. 'Every one of your employees was smiling . . . because of that I've decided to give you the business.'"[6] Parents are far less likely to recommend a school to others if their experiences are with a lot of unhappy employees.

Unfortunately, lobbying is required also. I can remember the year in California that the governor announced a percentage increase to all California school systems. Immediately, all employees begin to calculate their potential raise. However, this particular governor did not include any increase for transportation for the upcoming year. Is any school district going to be able to provide a cost-of-living adjustment for all employees except bus drivers? Of course not. Lobbying is a necessary aspect of increasing income, or games are played that hurt students. How are the bus drivers given the same raise as everyone else? It usually comes out of instruction. So, in a multitude of ways, increasing income is a key responsibility of the finance office.

Finance Question 4

Finance question 4 is, "Can the district document that fewer resources (time and money) are spent operating the finance system?" I have worked in school districts where one signature on a purchase order was sufficient and in another district where up to seven signatures were required on certain purchase orders. The principal, the federal projects coordinator, the assistant superintendent for instruction, two business officials, the superintendent, and the board president signed for purchases. Employees knew that they better not expect any requested item to arrive before the end of the school year.

I have written in chapter 8 details of the responsibility to reduce costs per pupil for noninstructional activities. The finance office may head up this initiative or it may come from the leader in operations. In order to answer yes to question 4, however, both time and money must be reduced. Therefore, I will speak only to reducing time in this chapter.

I think the only job description necessary for a school secretary is "smile when interrupted." If it's not staff and students, it is a parent or somebody from the district office. Sometimes even the principals have a second to speak with their school secretary. One key responsibility is to determine the number of hours per week various people are spending on financial obligations. It can be assumed that the people working in the finance office are spending 100 percent of their time, but what about teachers, secretaries, curriculum staff, principals? The next and all-important responsibility of the finance office is to reduce this time. By looking at these four questions, it can easily be seen that the job of finance is to have much more accurate information for decision makers in finance, have more income, spend less on noninstructional line items (chapter 8), and use less time to accomplish all of this. Technology may be a big help. For example, if a school board or superintendent really does need multiple signatures on each purchase order, then each of the people who must sign the purchase order needs a scanner to scan the bar code on the purchase order. Since so much time is wasted attempting to track down the purchase orders with all of these steps, let the person who ordered the supply go online and track the progress, just like can be done with shipping companies. I realize this may be impractical. In reality, I'm not expecting the scanners, but with a yes answer to the operations questions and a yes answer to the first three finance questions, district officials should feel much more secure spending less time on financial operations. "There's too much waste in banking," says Carl Reichardt. "Getting rid of it takes tenacity, not brilliance."[7] Kaplan and Norton write, "If anything, eliminating waste time in a service delivery process is even more important than in manufacturing companies, since consumers are increasingly intolerant of being forced to wait in line for services."[8] Deming says, "Unnecessary paperwork is a serious loss. A lot of it originates in management's supposition that the cure for repetition of a mistake or fraud is more audits, more inspection."[9] District officials need to have evidence that less time is spent on finance, in addition to the fact that the superintendent, chief financial officer, and board all have a better handle on the budget and overall finances.

NOTES

1. Webber and Wallace, 95.
2. Karen Berman and Joe Knight, *Financial Intelligence* (Boston, MA: Harvard Business School Press, 2006), 4.
3. Berman and Knight, 33.
4. Berman and Knight, 23.
5. Kaplan and Norton, 64.
6. Burlingham, 78.
7. Carl Reichardt quoted in Collins, 128.
8. Kaplan and Norton, 118.
9. Deming, *The New Economics*, 22.

8

OPERATIONS AND BUILDINGS

In order for the school board to be successful, the superintendent must be successful. In order for the school superintendent to be successful, the noninstructional operations must operate smoothly at less cost.

School leaders have in their minds opportunities they would like to offer their students. Most of these possibilities cost money and, except for a few grants from foundations, the money comes from taxes. Therefore, there is pushback from citizens, including educators, who believe they are already paying enough in taxes. Often educators hear the advice to cut back on the visible—conferences, staff development, and field trips. The first question in this chapter is about cutting back on the invisibles so that visible items can be increased. Less money on trash pickup and more on music instruments is the basic idea. The opposite of what school districts want to achieve was reported by *Education Week* regarding Los Angeles's payroll issues.[1] The increased cost for payroll and consultants to fix software glitches is not where education money should be spent.

When automobile experts want to compare car manufacturers, they have determined the constants. In spite of differing currency, salaries, and shipping costs, car manufacturers can be compared in two basic ways: (1) the number of warranty repairs per hundred cars and (2) the number of hours to manufacture a car. Education has no such common denominator in normal operating practice. "Almost every industry has an association or trade group that sets quality standards against which companies can measure the quality of their products."[2] What should this measuring basic be in education? The premise of this chapter is that it should simply be the annual cost per pupil for each district's noninstructional operations.

Operations Question 1

Question 1 for operations is, "Has the school system calculated the cost per pupil for each noninstructional operation?"

The three reasons for calculating cost per pupil for each operation are (1) baseline data, (2) ability to learn from other school districts, and (3) cost per pupil captures the emotions of everyone.

In any effort to improve all systems, baseline data is the place to start. Prior to any change discussions, leaders need baseline data. Where are we now? The answer is neither good nor bad; it just is! Transportation wants to calculate the cost per mile, and custodial services wants to calculate cost per square foot, and I argue, "No." The place to start is cost per pupil for all operations. What is the cost per pupil for our substitute calling process? What is the cost per pupil for providing substitutes for the county jury system? What is the cost per pupil for home to school transportation? What is the cost per pupil for liability insurance? What is the cost per pupil for labor negotiations? What is the cost per pupil for printing of noninstructional materials?

It may take a year or longer for an organization to agree on all of the noninstructional components of operating a school district and then to define what is included in each calculation. The first decision is the number of pupils, as this number changes daily. I suggest using the official number used by the state.

The second decision is what to include in cost per pupil. Printing is an example. Costs include the total cost for print shop employees; equipment purchase and leases; paper, toner, and ink; and outside printing. I have spoken to a person who calculated the cost for electricity for each page printed, but this is way too precise for most school systems. What is needed is a reasonable cost for all printing services.

Just like cost per pupil for printing, all operations have many different contributing factors. This is why it is reasonable to expect these calculations to take a year; people have full-time jobs in addition to making these decisions and calculations. The baseline numbers are crucial, and there is no need to rush the definitions for each department.

Operations Question 2

Once cost per pupil is calculated for each noninstructional operation, districts are ready for question 2, "Is each operation testing at least one hypothesis to reduce costs (without reducing quality of service)?" It is a little more complicated than saying each department must have a data collection system in place. Data from each department will be collected at different intervals depending upon the department and the hypothesis. However, in most cases data should be collected at least monthly.

The key words are "testing theories." Sir James Dyson said, "I made 5,127 prototypes of my vacuum before I got it right. There were 5,126 failures. But I learned from each one. That's how I came up with a solution. So, I don't mind failure."[3] School districts need environments in which they can test out their ideas without fear of failure. If everyone knew how to reduce cost per pupil for trash pickup services, then everyone would already be doing it. The point is we don't all know and we must continually test out our ideas to see if they improve. "Fortune favors the experimental mind."[4] "The process of searching for answers is more important than having an answer."[5]

Two examples of testing ideas come from Jenks, Oklahoma, schools. They are (1) cost per month to replace broken glass caused by lawnmowers kicking up rocks and (2) cost per month for workers' compensation claims for food services. Each department agreed upon what they wanted to improve and regularly went about testing out hypotheses to reduce costs.

Another example is excess printing to compensate for lack of time to count out the precise number of students in each classroom. Assume a school has 500 pupils and a flyer is to be sent home with each student. How many flyers are actually printed? It could be between 600 and 700 because nobody has the time to count out the exact number of flyers per classroom. The print shop can experiment with ways to lower the extra printing costs and still have flyers for each student. How do professional printers count? They do it by weight. Would the cost of such an accurate scale be offset by the savings in paper and ink? If students did the weighing, would there be educational value? Let's experiment at one or two schools to see if the excess printing can be reduced. Eventually, this experiment could be repeated throughout the school district and show up as a reduction in cost per pupil for printing. The print shop could easily calculate the percentage of overage that is reduced.

In these examples, the department heads in landscaping, food services, and printing can answer yes to question 2. They can describe the hypotheses they are testing and show the periodic graphs. The question at this point is not "Did you reduce costs?" but "Did you have a hypothesis you were testing over the course of a year and can you show me the results of your experiment?" Leaders should never forget that many have "learned that focusing upon quality actually reduced cost more than focusing only on cost."[6]

Operations Question 3

The third question is more difficult: Is each operation testing hypotheses to increase quality of service (without increasing costs)? Quality of service can be ascertained through inspection and through surveys. Both have merit. The only added value I want to bring to the decision-making process is random selection. It is impossible to have 100 percent inspection in schools or to receive a thoughtful response from 100 percent of the students, parents, or staff.

The solution is random sampling. If we do not use random sampling, we are victims of the loudest voices. The custodians clean the classrooms where the teachers complain, for example. First I will describe random sampling with inspection and then with feedback from staff.

Custodians have a prescribed number of stations to clean and have a list of the jobs to be completed. The custodians have an administrator who is responsible for supervising their work. The random sampling for inspection works this way:

1. Write down the precise responsibilities of each custodian with exact locations.
2. On a regular basis, randomly select one location to visit.
3. Keep track of locations that meet standards and those that do not.

I realize the inspection process I described could be used as a component of evaluation. My purpose is not improved evaluations, but development of a consistent measure of quality of service. Our goal is to reduce costs and at the very least not reduce the quality of service because of reduced costs. Further, many great employees will welcome this method of inspection because their boss will see all of their good work, not just the occasional problem that is reported to the boss. Instead of "this is the third time this month I've had a complaint about you," it is, "I realize we have had three complaints, but of the last fifty random inspections I have only found one area that needed improvement."

The car manufacturers have an annual number for quality; it is the number of warranty repairs per 100 cars. I suggest school districts have the same number each year. How many cleaning inspections per 100 were unsatisfactory?

A feedback system from staff could be used instead of the inspection process. It would work in a similar way. The difference is each randomly selected employee would answer questions(s). When each employee is given a questionnaire, sometimes only the loudest voices will respond. Random selection solves this issue. With random selection, each selected person is monitored to be sure results are turned in. The question(s) need to be very simple, for example:

Please read the cleaning requirements for classroom and shared space. In your opinion, is the custodial staff:

Table 8.1. Cleaning Requirements for Classroom and Shared Space

	My space	Shared space
1. Completing their duties less than 90 percent of the time?		
2. Completing their duties 90–100 percent of the time?		
3. Completing their duties over 98 percent of the time plus other helpful tasks?		
If you checked #1 or #3, give specifics.		

The random selection for feedback works this way:

1. How many staff are customers of the custodians? Let's assume seventy-five.
2. Determine the number of staff the principal can realistically gather information from on a regular basis. Let's assume two.
3. Determine the number of weeks during the school year the principal can accomplish gathering the data. Let's assume thirty.
4. Randomly select the two people to interview each week.

Again, the purpose is to have an annual number for custodial services. Out of 100 responses in the district, how many checked #3?

Operations Question 4

The fourth question sums up the purpose of this chapter. "Is there evidence over several years that overall operations has decreased the annual cost per pupil and increased the quality of service?" Even though I have separated quality and cost for purposes of delineating thoughts, in reality, "there can be no talk of price without a simultaneous measure of quality."[7]

School districts must know that overall cost per pupil for operations has been reduced and the quality of service has increased. Additionally, they need to have this data for each and every operation. When a school district can show over several years that operations are less expensive and satisfaction levels are up, they have accomplished a minor miracle.

Every church I have attended collects money for missionaries serving in other countries. Only one church, however, made a direct connection to every donation. Everyone knows that a basic budget is needed for salaries, housing, airfare, and so forth. However, when a church exceeds its pledge for the basics, what then? In one church, a committee selected particular items to purchase once the basic amount had been received. On a regular basis, thank-you notes came to the congregation from all over the world. We felt connected.

Likewise, the members of the support staff need to feel connected. "Often employees do not see how their efforts help the organization succeed. Similarly, employees cannot see how the business's success relates to them."[8] My suggestion is that teachers submit requests for instructional materials, field trips, children's author visits, and so on to a committee of support staff members. These employees are able to spend their savings on instructional support. If these employees figure out a way to save money on any operation and if they are allowed to spend their savings on student learning, they will clearly see how their efforts relate to learning.

NOTES

1. Trotter, 1.
2. Webber and Wallace, 11.
3. Salter, 44.
4. DuFour, DuFour, Eaker, and Kaharnek, xv.
5. DuFour, DuFour, Eaker, and Kaharnek, 4.
6. Liker, 25.
7. Deming, *Some Theory of Sampling*, 13.
8. Michelli, 20.

THE STUDENT
LEARNING

9

PROCESS (FORMATIVE) DATA

In order for the school board to be successful, the superintendent must be successful. In order for the school superintendent to be successful, the instructional staff, including all teachers and principals, must always know if learning is occurring at an appropriate rate for students to meet end-of-year standards.

Process data, or the word most commonly used by educators—formative data—is merely data collected all throughout the year to determine if students are going to meet the end-of-the-year standards. If this were a business book, the language would be "quality assurance attempts to head off problems at the pass by tweaking a production process until it can produce a quality product."[1]

Process Data Question 1

Process data question 1: Is every student informed on the first day of every course about precisely what they will learn in the course? Nothing takes the place of up-front informing students precisely what they are going to learn. "School leaders can add value to standards by taking the state documents and recreating them with greater precision, focus and prioritization."[2] In Maconaquah School

Corporation (Indiana), teacher Dan McCaulley led the effort to provide students both state standards and then precise concepts to learn. Under each standard appropriate for a grade level, numbered key concepts were inserted. The state standards were outlined, and not numbered, to separate them from what students are expected to know. What students are to learn is divided into what students will know and what they will be able to do at the end of the course. I am not suggesting a syllabus, but a detailed description of learning outcomes. Video and still images may be necessary to convey the expectations. Actual students can be very helpful also. For example, a first-grade teacher can invite a boy and a girl from second grade to read to the new first graders. These two are average readers who could read very little the first week of first grade a year ago. Now, they are reading approximately sixty words a minute with first-grade text. The incoming first graders can hear what they will sound like in nine months.

Why is this first step so important? Educators want students to focus on learning and not gamesmanship. In a Missouri seminar, I asked teachers to indicate if they were very able to psych out their professors in college. They knew exactly what would be forthcoming on exams and memorized only that content. I inquired of one teacher precisely her method; how could she accomplish such a feat? The reply was that she was in a study group. By design, 50 percent of the study time was spent sharing collective insights regarding the uniqueness of the professor. His or her interests, special expertise, and clues to what was really important were all catalogued. The other 50 percent of the time was spent cramming. What a great plan for gaining good grades and what a poor plan for actual learning!

Providing students with only a textbook is inadequate for at least two reasons: (1) most textbooks, by design, are focused upon what students are to know without balancing what they are to be able to do and (2) students are unable to discern between what is nice to know and what is essential to know. Schmoker italicizes this point: "carefully select and teach *only the most essential standards*."[3] It is crucial that teams of educators use textbooks, standards, and experience to prepare these precise learning expectations. It is perfectly fine to teach trivia; it is fun and interesting. However, students are not evaluated on trivia. Their grades are based upon learning the essential content provided them on the first day of class.

When preparing these learning expectations, placing content within strands is very helpful. All of these classifications assist students in filing away the content in their long-term memory.

Some parents and students will need assistance with feelings of being overwhelmed when first provided learning expectations for a whole year. Some will panic and think they must learn all of this content in a week. These parents and students cannot be blamed, as they are used to learning a chapter at a time. It is extremely rare to find a parent who cannot understand the power of laying out the year's learning expectations the first week of school, but I would never say such a parent cannot be found. The preponderance of parents appreciate this approach so they can assist their children on convenient schedules.

Process Data Question 2

Process data question 2: Do teachers and principals receive weekly feedback on learning progress toward end-of-the-year expectations in all classes? Are the three basic classroom graphs (class/student run chart, histogram, and scatter diagram) in place in over 90 percent of the classrooms?

Teachers are leaders of classrooms, and principals are leaders of schools. Unless the leaders have weekly feedback on students' progress toward *end-of-the-year* learning expectations, they cannot lead. Teachers and principals can fulfill many of their management responsibilities without this feedback, but they cannot lead. End-of-the-year is emphasized here because education is used to having only data on chapter tests. Think about it: Students are accountable for their short-term memory (chapter tests), and educators are accountable for students' long-term memory (standardized tests). "No number of successes in short-term problems will ensure long-term success."[4] Without this basic feedback, teachers and principals rely upon anecdotal evidence which is a "form of guessing."[5] Walter She-whart wrote in the 1930s, "the only reason to carry out a test is to improve a process, to improve the quality and quantity of the next run or the next year's crop."[6] The next "run" for education is the next unit of instruction and the next "year's crop" is next year's students.

The statement above is based upon Marcus Buckingham's distinction between leadership and management.[7] Management is meeting the unique needs of individuals, and leadership is meeting the needs all have in common. Since all students need to meet the course learning expectations, teacher-leaders and principal-leaders need to know their progress at any moment in time. Weekly process (formative) data is the foundation of this leadership. Schmoker states, "We don't commonly see teaching, followed by assessment, then adjustment to practice on the basis of assessment results."[8] "Statistics allow you to determine which processes or parts of processes are causing your company the most problems."[9] The purpose of using process (formative) data is to solve issues before the final results are posted.

I have asked the interview question, "Why do you want to be a teacher?" to hundreds of teacher applicants. Never have I received the answer, "I want to help students with their short-term memory." Teachers desire to impact the student now and far into the future. Thirty-six unrelated chapter tests are not the vehicle for the desired long-term positive influence upon the lives of students. Teachers must assess on a weekly basis end-of-the-year expectations. Students, teachers, and principals must know if adequate progress is being made. Educators need to "look in the mirror at what we are doing right now, always with the expectation of making discernible progress in the short and long term."[10] Figure 9.1 is a blank student run chart. Students graph their progress each week toward end-of-the-year expectations and can tell if they are on track to meet 100 percent of the expectations by year's end.

Figure 9.2, "Class Run Chart," is a slight variation of figure 9.1. This run chart for the whole classroom has a sloping line that begins at 30 percent and ends at 89 percent. Why? Because in this classroom, 30 percent of the formative assessment questions are questions from prior courses/grades, and last year's students ended the year with 88 percent correct. Students are expected to remember the content from prior courses and have a goal of outperforming last year's students. The 30 percent and the 89 percent are not arbitrary numbers pulled out of the air.

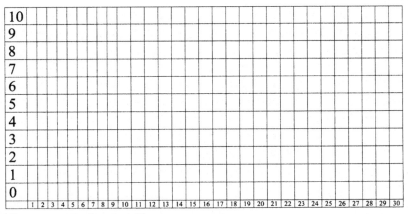

Figure 9.1.   Student Run Chart

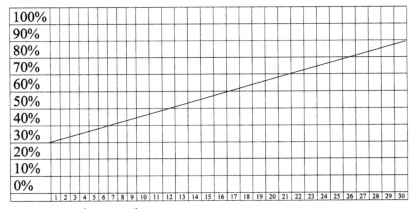

Figure 9.2.   Class Run Chart

For example, an eighth-grade science course could have the policy that all nongraded formative quizzes will be 70 percent eighth-grade science, 15 percent seventh-grade science, and 15 percent sixth-grade science. The first week of school, the expectation is that students would answer all of the sixth- and seventh-grade questions correctly and none of the eighth-grade questions. The goal is to have continuous improvement so the students can exceed the learning results of the prior year's eighth graders.

I described in detail in *Improving Student Learning* the precise process for the weekly quizzes, but I will summarize here.[11] Of course there is no time to administer end-of-the-year finals each and every week. Such a plan would leave no time for teaching. So if formative assessment on only the just-taught chapter is useless and there is no time for assessing complete knowledge of end-of-the-year content, what do educators do? They use sampling techniques.

To continue the eighth-grade science example, assume the sixth-, seventh-, and eighth-grade teachers agreed upon 100 essential science concepts for each grade level. The appropriate sample size for the weekly quiz is ten questions per week (square root of total questions in eighth grade) and then a couple of sixth-grade questions and a couple of seventh-grade questions for a total of fourteen. The content to be quizzed is selected randomly from the total list of concepts. It is the randomness that makes the data accurate, as students cannot psych out random selection. The total correct (or percentage correct) are graphed by student, by classroom, by grade level/department, and by school. Students complete all student graphs and as often as possible complete the graphing for the classroom, grade level, and school. In Lexington, Nebraska, Julie Otero, the district's curriculum director, even posts weekly the total for all eight schools on a district run chart.

"Psychologists tell us that we share certain fundamental needs—the need to feel successful in our work, the need to feel a sense of belonging, and the need to live a life of significance by making a difference."[12] The classroom and school run charts communicate, without words, the contribution of everyone. Students know their results and know how they contributed to the total growth of the classroom and even the whole school. Senge writes, "You cannot have a learning community without a shared vision. Without a pull toward some goal which people truly want to achieve, the forces in support of the status quo can be overwhelming."[13] These simple lists of learning outcomes and the three simple charts go a long way toward changing the classroom into a learning community with a shared vision. "American management must still learn that in order to compete, they must learn to cooperate."[14] Students experiencing this simple use of process data are learning at an early age that in order to compete (outperform prior students) they have to cooperate as a class, grade level, and school. Sue Winter, high-school economics teacher (John Marshall High School, Rochester, Minnesota) reports that her seniors, weeks from graduation, work hard to outperform prior semesters of students. They experience, of all places in an economics class, that cooperation is necessary in order to be more competitive.

In order for school districts to answer yes to question 2, the vast majority of teachers must have this regular feedback. Not all feedback must be weekly, however. It is most common for feedback on background knowledge to be weekly and feedback on performance to be given less often. I often see feedback on reading fluency given weekly in Title I and special education but monthly in general education. Some districts assess math problem solving and writing bi-weekly. Art projects are not usually assessed on a firm timetable, but when the particular assignments are due. Of course, block scheduling speeds up any timetables I have described here.

Peter Senge quotes Shell Oil's Arie de Gues, who states that "organizational learning occurs in three ways: through teaching, through 'changing the rules of the game,' and through play. Play is the most rare and potentially the most powerful."[15] The use of process data described above clearly needs good teaching, the rules of the game are changed in a number of ways, and the process is great fun for students and faculty.

I will conclude these comments on the need for regular feedback with a Schmoker quote. "Every parent was given an expensive, multifold, grade-by-grade list of what children would be taught. We (parents) were emphatically assured that our children would learn

Scatter Diagram									
10								++	+++
9							+++		++
8					++		++	+	++++
7			+				++	++++	++
6		+		++	+		+++++	+++	++++
5	+	+	+		+++	++++		++	+++
4			+	+++	++++++	+++	+++++	++++	+
3	++		++	++++++ +	++	+++++ +++	+	+++	
2	++	++	++++++	+++++	+++++	+++		+	
1	+++++	+++++ ++++	++++++	++	+		++		
0	++++++ ++++	+++++ ++	+++	+		++			
	1	2	3	4	5	6	7	8	9

Number Correct

Quiz Number

Figure 9.3. Scatter Diagram

these standards, that the schools were organized to teach them. But a group of us (including some educational researchers) made an interesting discovery: that there wasn't the slightest resemblance between those lists and what our children were taught."[16] My additional comments are that it is a big waste of money to expensively print the list of standards to be learned. Why? While the parents should have the list, the most important recipient of the list is students. Added to each item should be a box to write the date that the standard was first taught and a means of recording success in learning the standard. Some teachers use check marks, but the means preferred by students is to use multicolored markers to highlight every standard that has been learned.

The second aspect of question 2 speaks to the quality of the graphs. So far I have described the simple run (line) graph. Also needed is the scatter diagram, as it displays a dot for each student on each assessment. Education is used to average scores that hide the fact that some students are failing to achieve the intended outcomes.[17] The same can be said for a run chart that adds up the total or percentage correct for a whole classroom, grade level, course, or school. The scatter diagram is very simply a dot for each student and each assessment. Figure 9.3 is an example of a scatter diagram. There is a dot for each student for each weekly nongraded quiz. When I first heard of the scatter diagram in 1992, I assumed this was a great tool for the teacher, but it was not to be seen by students. I did not want to embarrass slower students. However, after fifteen years of sharing the three basic tools, teachers have convinced me I was wrong: Students love the scatter diagram. Even the slower students love seeing their contribution to the overall progress of the classroom.

The third basic chart is the histogram, shown in figure 9.4. In the beginning of the year, students and staff need to see the L-shaped histogram signifying that the students do not know the course content. A bell-shaped curve the first week of school documents low standards or students arriving better prepared than expected. Throughout the year, students enjoy seeing the L change to a bell shape and finally into a J. In some classrooms, teachers find students love having blank histograms in their data folders so they can look at the classroom scatter

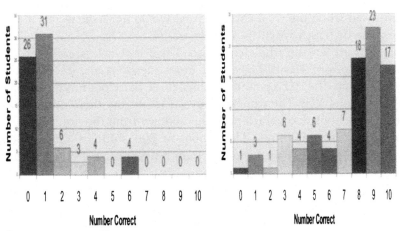

Figure 9.4. L to J Histogram

diagram and shade in the classroom histogram. Even in high school, they will look back at the movement from the L to the J.

The combination of aligned goals and continual measurement of progress toward meeting end-of-year expectations is powerful.

Process Data Question 3

Process data question 3: Is there a culture of celebrating ATBs (all-time bests) by student, classroom, grade level, department, and school? Do the teachers and principals see the school as a contest factory or as a joyful place constantly celebrating learning? Every reader knows the contest mentality—a limited number of As, which classroom has the most PTA members, who can sell the most magazine subscriptions, and who can win the science fair. The false belief is that the losers are motivated to do better next time. Pressure is on educators, who are given continual contest ideas from society. Some influential parents want more children to be losers so their children can be winners.

The ATB (all-time best) leadership style recognizes the basic human needs to (1) know that I am improving and (2) know that I contributed to a successful team. In the previous science example, if a student's prior best was five of fourteen correct, he/she is naturally enthused when the total correct is six. We do not have to teach students to be happy when they improve.

ATBs are for the whole class also. The science classroom outperforms its prior ATB of 103 by seven more questions correct. The girls' soccer team lifts 2,125 pounds, twenty-three more pounds more than the previous ATB. The students only waste seventy-three minutes, as a whole school, due to tardiness; this is down from the previous ATB of eighty-three minutes. The school of 500 students reads 7,386 words in a minute, up from last month's ATB of 6,478 words per minute.

The list can go on and on, but process data question 3 is only asking, "Is there a culture of celebrating ATBs in the school and school system?" Are students, administrators, and district office staff always congratulating students in their continuous improvement? ATBs are not bribes: "If you have an ATB in writing you can watch a video." They are genuine thank-yous mixed with fun and humor. Examples of ways teachers celebrate ATBs always match their personality: a ding on the teacher bell (Iowa high-school science), barking like a seal (Nebraska high-school math), calling in the principal (South Carolina elementary), a dance (North Carolina elementary), a cheer (Minnesota elementary), a starburst on the class graph (California high-school history), and even the teacher standing on the teacher desk, as if in a parade, and throwing Tootsie Rolls (Minnesota middle school). "The case for generating a steady stream of short-term team 'wins' is not new and is pure common sense. If anything, it is mystifying that schools have yet to institute structures that allow people to see that their hard work is paying off—this week or this month—not next year or five years from now."[18]

Much has been eloquently written and spoken regarding professional learning communities. The power of teachers and administrators looking at student results from common assessments and common assignments can not be overstated. We must not, however, overlook the power of the learning community being the teacher with his/her students. When students see the run chart showing weekly progress, the scatter diagram with a dot for each student each week, and the histogram moving from the L shape through the bell to the J, they are an excited team. Students also have ideas regarding what can improve learning.

"All of the qualities that have been traditionally and erroneously applied to competition actually apply better to cooperation. Cooperation builds character, is basic to human nature, and makes learning more enjoyable and productive."[19] The basic graphs and ensuing celebrations of ATBs are evidence of classroom cooperation at its best.

Process Data Question 4

Process data question 4: Are students and staff actively involved in establishing hypotheses they can test out for the improvement of learning? Once the curriculum chapter questions and first three process data questions can be answered in the affirmative, school systems are ready to create a culture of continually testing hypotheses to see what brings about improvement in their respective classrooms, schools, and districts/divisions. Is there a culture of experimentation? Every time I have seen a classroom run chart, three patterns emerge: incline, valley, and plateau. When inclines occur, we celebrate the ATBs. When valleys occur, we merely discuss what happened. Valleys are caused by poor attendance, distracting events, or bad luck. Bad luck occurs when the random selection of concepts creates more difficult items. The first example of this type of formative data took place in 1992 with students charting growth in geography.[20] They were expected to know the location of fifty U.S. states and fifty other locations (mountains, rivers, cities, and lakes). One week, by pure random selection, no states were chosen. The graph took a big dip because the nonstates were more difficult for the students to learn.

Plateaus, or flat lines, as they are sometimes called, always happen. What now? The process is to involve the team in establishing hypotheses. What can we do to start our learning on another incline? The team can be the students and their teacher, a team of grade level or department teachers, the principal and teachers, or a district/division administrator plus school administrators and teacher-leaders. A yes for question 4 means the educators, when faced with a plateau, do not blame others and do not rush out to purchase yet another program. The teachers do not blame the students, the administrators do not blame the teachers, and the school board does not blame the staff. All say, "We have good people" who need another strategy to bring about improvement. With process data students, teachers, and principals can know in a few weeks if their improvement strategy shows promise. The point is that the flat line is not met with yet another mandate but is met with a team meeting to determine the next hypothesis.

NOTES

1. Webber and Wallace, 11.
2. Douglas B. Reeves, *The Leader's Guide to Standards* (San Francisco: John Wiley and Sons, 2002), 8.
3. Schmoker, 125.
4. Deming, *The New Economics*, 25.
5. Webber and Wallace, 109.
6. Walter A. Shewhart, *Statistical Method from the Viewpoint of Quality Control* (Mineola, NY: Dover Press, 1986); reproduced in Cecilia S. Kilian, *The World of W. Edwards Deming* (Knoxville, TN: SPC Press, 1992), 98.
7. Marcus Buckingham, *The One Thing You Need to Know* (New York: Simon and Schuster, 2005).
8. Schmoker, 24.
9. Webber and Wallace, 14.
10. DuFour, DuFour, Eaker, and Kaharnek, xv.
11. Jenkins, *Improving Student Learning*, 71–98.
12. DuFour, DuFour, Eaker, and Kaharnek, 6.
13. Senge, 209.
14. Deming, *The New Economics*, 56.
15. Senge, 315.
16. Schmoker, 33.
17. DuFour, DuFour, Eaker, and Kaharnek, 23.
18. Schmoker, 122.
19. Deming, *The New Economics*, 152.
20. Jenkins, *Improving Student Learning*, 37–43.

10

RESULTS (SUMMATIVE) DATA

In order for the school board to be successful, the superintendent must be successful. In order for the school superintendent to be successful, the board, all employees, and any interested community members must be able to easily look at trend data to determine where the school district's students have improved.

I always wanted to answer press questions regarding an increase in achievement by telling the reporter, "I have no clue why our test scores went up; there is a 50 percent chance we were lucky." I never did because I'd have on my hands a lot of very mad, hard-working, talented teachers. However, because the reporter only had data for this year and for last year, it is a true statement. This year's third graders are different people from last year's third graders. Therefore, a decrease or increase could be caused by program improvement or by the fact that different students were tested.

Results Data Question 1

So results question 1 is, "Are all data reported as a pattern or trend over a minimum of five years?" When teachers state that one cannot compare third graders to third graders, they are right. However, one can compare third grade to third grade to third grade to third grade to third grade. A trend begins to develop in three years, but systems must be able to report data over a five-year period of time in order to eliminate luck from the data. It is highly unlikely that a school system with continual improvement over a period of five years was lucky for five years, meaning that for five years in a row students arrived more prepared.

Those who wish to punish educators with data do not need five years of data; they only need one year's data to rank and embarrass people. "Ranking is a farce. Apparent performance is actually attributable mostly to the system that the individual works in, not to the individual himself . . . Ranking comes from failure to understand variation from common causes . . . The ranking of people indicates abdication of management."[1]

Those who wish to communicate true improvement must display trend data. I recognize that many of the results in school districts are from state-administered exams. Usually, state boards of education change the testing process before a five-year trend can be established. When I have spoken to members of state legislatures and state boards, I have always recommended that the exams and processes stay firm for ten years. There will always be ways to tweak the dates, exams, suppliers, and so on, but school systems desperately need the trend data that comes from consistent leadership.

That said, there are many sets of data in school systems that are not dependent upon any state agency. Schools all over the United States are measuring reading fluency in the primary grades. What percent of students have met the district's fluency rate standards for the past five years? Is this percent by school or for the school district as a whole? Schools have discipline records. What is the average number of referrals to the office for discipline for each of the past five years? Or better yet, what percent of students met the district's standard for acceptable behavior? (This could be zero or one discipline referral for the year.) What percent of the students in Advanced Placement courses score a three or higher on the Advanced Placement exams? What is the trend over the past five years?

School district leaders meeting with their state representatives in the legislature and state school board will have a much stronger case for requesting constant data when they can show five-year trend data for everything under their control. Just like it is hard to lobby against incentive pay for teachers when school systems hand out approximately 10,000 incentives (5 per day times 180 days times 13 years) to children, it hard to argue for trend data from the state when no trend data is collected for locally controlled data.

With data we must distinguish between growth and development. Ackoff writes, "Growth is an increase in size or number. Development is an increase in capability, competence."[2] This chapter is all about development and not growth. In fact, I hope readers have the personnel office of their school district remove all references to rank in their state according to enrollment. "Come work for us; we are the third-largest district in _____ (state)" is meaningless. It implies we are smarter because of our enrollment and if you come to work for us you will naturally become smarter also.

Results Data Question 2

When school systems can say yes to question 1 and prove they have five-year trend data for every set of data they regularly keep, they are ready for question 2. Results data question 2 is, "Are the five basic graphs (run, radar, correlation, control chart, and Pareto) used to analyze and communicate all end-of-the-year results data?" I will describe these graphs one at a time. Together they give a complete picture of analysis for any school system. None of the charts collect averages, but all collect percent proficient. "Avoid using the average, or arithmetic mean, in understanding test scores."[3]

The acronym PGA can help us remember the sequence with the use of data: perception, graphs, and analysis. Raw numbers and experience can provide a perception, but leaders have a responsibility to dig further with graphs. Giuliani writes, "I love to visualize charts, so much so that my staff would jokingly call me 'Chart Boy' when they thought I wasn't listening."[4] The last step is analysis. For professors reading the documents, my recommendation is that the heart of the statistics class for the master's degree should be the graphs, and the heart of the statistics class for the doctorate should be the analysis. The course for the doctorate is appropriate—the analysis tools necessary to write a dissertation. However, the master's degree course should be about success on the job, and the graphs are what are needed.

"True professionals are not 'always positive.' Instead, they radiate competence, capability, and expertise by being serious and self-assured."[5] The data is not always positive, but the five charts described in this chapter radiate competence, capability, and expertise.

I remember being in a school district listening to the assessment staff complain that the principals never looked at all the data they provided, so I looked at the binders full of data provided to each principal. I really do not see how anybody could make sense of those pages and pages of data in column after column. One principal called it "datarrhea" and said nobody in his district was cleaning it up. It is the responsibility of senior leadership to ensure that school site staffs have data that provide them insight. It is not the job of principals to take the raw data and make sense of it for their teachers.

The first chart I call the chamber of commerce graph. This chamber of commerce view answers the simple question, "Did the school district improve?" I am not inferring negatives about the chamber of commerce. The members have businesses to operate and generally do not have time to look at the school district's data. They do want, however, a simple answer to the question, "Did the schools improve last year?" It is one dot per year for all district assessments. Such a simple graph makes little sense to educators as it combines all end-of-the-year assessments into one number. Yes, all reading, all math, all science, all history/social science, and any other end-of-course assessments into one number. The question is, "On what percent of end-of-course assessments did students score proficient or advanced?" It is very encouraging to share with the public and school board a trend line of continuous improvement. Note that I am not suggesting that leaders pull numbers out of the air for the next year's goal, but that they remain firm in their commitment to continuously improve over prior years. "No matter what you're tracking, comparing results to previous indicators, then demanding improvement, is the best way to achieve anything."[6] Figure 10.1 is from Rochester, Indiana, and was created prior to the retirement of Superintendent Bob Poffenbarger, who served as the district superintendent for twenty years.

It is also important for principals to have the exact same chamber of commerce chart for their schools. Staffs need to see, as a team, that their efforts are paying dividends. When staffs see data only a subject at a time, they do not all feel like the school is a team working together for improvement. We know that counselors, special education staff, and all other teachers contribute knowledge that might be assessed in any core subject. The chamber of commerce chart gives the team picture.

The second chart for results (summative) data is the radar chart, sometimes called the spider chart or web chart. It provides the details that are not visible with the one-line chart. "Ultimately the leader does not need to know who beat whom, but only the percentage of students who meet or exceed standards."[7] The radar chart is perfect for displaying this information for multiple years and multi-

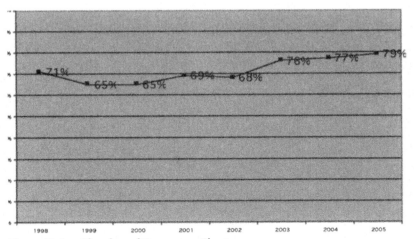

Figure 10.1. Chamber of Commerce Chart

ple assessments on one sheet of paper. Every end-of-course assessment has a vector on the radar chart. Multiple years can be shown on the radar chart with up to fifty or more different assessments. When large numbers of vectors are present, it is wise to print on 11 × 17 paper. When school boards have been through the annual PowerPoint presentation with an overload of different slides, each showing results from one exam, they are thrilled with the opportunity to see all results from the past five years on one sheet of paper.

Figure 10.2 is an Excel-created radar chart from Cecil County, Maryland, simplified by Michael Schmook. Only the line from the most recent year is left, a double asterisk is typed adjacent to all exams with an all-time best, and the state goal (AMO) is included. Thus one can see growth over time, annual results, and accountability measures. When people first see the radar chart, their eyes cross. They do not think anyone would be serious about such a graph, but in just a minute or two of careful analysis people understand it and

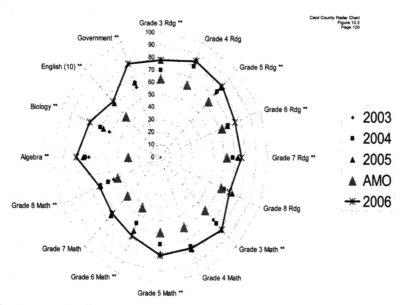

Figure 10.2.   Cecil County Radar Chart Figure

see so much more about their system than could ever been gleaned from fifty different PowerPoint slides.

School systems need not limit their radar chart to exam results but can use it for annual results in discipline, attendance, participation in extracurricular activities, graduation rates, community service, and so on. All that is necessary is to have percentage data for every aspect that is measured. What percent of the students met our criteria for successful behavior? For successful attendance? Participated in at least one extracurricular activity? Completed their community service projects? Graduated? Deming wrote, "People are asking for better schools, with no clear idea how to improve education, nor even how to define improvement of education."[8] The radar chart is a start in defining improvement as multiple aspects over multiple years displayed on one page. Further, evidence of improvement or lack of improvement is easily discerned.

"Repeat business is probably the most basic measure of quality"[9] is a quote that can be posted everywhere. Attendance and graduation rates are certainly measures of "repeat business." In education, we will not use the phrase repeat business, but if students and parents are pleased with the quality of our school districts they will repeatedly come to school and will eventually graduate. Great businesses do lose customers sometimes, and great schools probably do not graduate everyone. However, many of the vectors on the radar chart can be studied through the lens of repeat business as the basic measure of quality.

The radar chart is the cover of school plans. My recommendation is that nothing should be included in a school plan that cannot be a vector on the radar chart. The same is true for the district's strategic plan. This will require rewriting the plans into a format which can be measured as percent success. If it is worth writing either in the district's strategic plan or in the school plan, then it is worth finding out if improvement occurred because of the plan and subsequent action. I concur with Schmoker's assessment of school plans and strategic planning: There is no evidence of improvement because of all of this work.[10] So one option is to throw them out, and the other option is to place a radar chart on the cover of each plan and become serious about tracking improvement. "When you measure quality statistically, you look for variation in a measurement between what the customer asks for and what you produce."[11] The radar chart shows at the outer edge what the customer asks for (all students successful) and what the school produced (the percentage of successful students).

"Every company has goals it wants to achieve, usually tied directly to revenue. Company goals are the result of a chain of activities or processes. However, each chain has a weak link that limits how much it can produce."[12] In education terms, every school district wants to create more and more graduates who meet high standards. However, every school district has at least one weak link that limits the number of graduates. The radar chart can give insight into the study of weak links. If the selected vectors are powerful enough, the weak links will become immediately visible.

When educators analyze both the one-line graph and the radar chart, they have a fairly good picture of district development. The three questions that might be answered are (1) Does the one-line, Chamber of Commerce, graph show improvement? (2) Where is the improvement? and maybe most important, (3) What interaction do we observe between the various aspects of the school district?

The first two charts are enumerative; the last three are analytical.

The third chart for results data is the correlation chart, created to compare process (formative) data with results (summative) data. Three columns in Excel are utilized. The first column is the students' names, the second column is a score from an instructional program in use in the school, and the third column is a score from an end-of-year assessment (often the state test). Excel has a command for a scatter diagram and has a function for the Pearson correlation coefficient. Most will say the correlation chart with a dot for each student is much more meaningful than the coefficient, but both together provide the most insight. School leaders need to know if their instructional dollars are bringing about improvement. I suggest using the process data from a district program just prior to the state assessment. In *The Balanced Scorecard*, the authors call this double-loop learning. "Double-loop learning occurs when managers question the underlying assumptions and reflect on whether the theory under which they were operating remains consistent with current evidence, observations, and experience. Of course, managers need feedback about whether the planned strategy remains a viable and successful strategy—the double-loop learning process. Managers need information so that they can question whether the fundamental assumptions made when they launched the strategy are valid."[13]

Figure 10.3 is a correlation chart comparing results from a district's state exam and the process data garnered from the weekly math quizzes as described in chapter 9. The chart shows a strong correlation (.72) between the process data and the results data. With this type of chart, district officials and teachers can be fairly certain that students who perform well on their process data are most likely going to score well on the state assessment.

The Pareto is the fourth chart; it is for item analysis. Tally marks work fine for item analysis, but the most powerful chart is the Pareto chart. In the Pareto chart from Cottonwood, Arizona, schools (figure 10.4), the students in the school made a total of 5,020 errors as noted in the upper left-hand corner. The errors were made in eight strands of reading with the most errors in elements of literature and the least number of errors in phonics. The curved line is cumulative errors; it

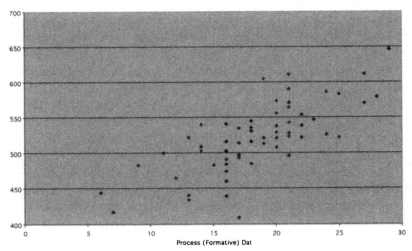

Figure 10.3. Correlation Chart

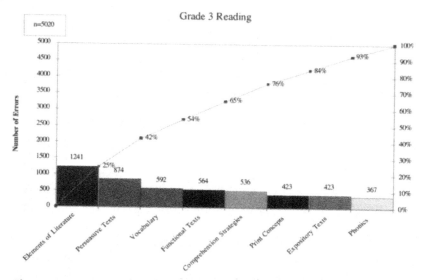

Figure 10.4. Pareto Chart from Cottonwood, Arizona, Schools

tells the reader where the greatest amount of effort should be placed to gain the most improvement in future years. For example, in figure 10.4, 54 percent of the errors came from three of the strands.

From looking at the Pareto chart, one cannot tell if there are more errors in elements of literature because there were more questions or because the students had a harder time learning this content. It doesn't matter. The goal is to reduce errors, and the Pareto chart displays errors. By the way, this is the most used graph at Toyota.[14]

The last chart is the control chart. Every time educators see ranked data, they should do their best to replace it with a control chart. Control charts were designed in the 1930s by Walter Shewhart to separate special-cause variation from common-cause variation.

The reason people invented statistics is because there is variation. If there were no variation, there would be no need for statistics. Some variation is common, and some is special. In fact, most variation among schools, school districts, states, and students is common. Students in fifth grade will typically read like an average fourth-, fifth-, or sixth-grader. This is common variation. Special variation is when a student in fifth grade reads like an average first grader or average eleventh grader.

Leaders need control charts to keep them from making poor decisions based upon ranked data. When data are ranked, people naturally assume first place and last place are special. Not necessarily so. A fifth-grade classroom's reading results could be ranked, providing the best and worst reader. However, if all are reading at the fourth-, fifth-, and sixth-grade levels, nobody is statistically special. All are special as human beings, but their reading ability is not special.

The control chart separates special from common variation. If a dot is placed on the control chart for each school in a larger district, staff can see which variation is special and which is common. They are treated differently. Special schools above the system should be studied to determine the reason for their success, and special schools below the system should be studied to provide extra assistance. "If one attribute stays between the upper and lower control limits on a consistent basis, the process is said to be *in control*. If the attribute goes above the upper control limit or below the lower control limit, the process is said to be *out of control*."[15] All the schools between the two lines (figure 10.5) are in the common range. Their differences are minor; these schools are within the system. If leaders are not happy with the results from these schools, pressure on them is inappropriate. These schools are within the system and are performing within the confines of the system. All of them need to be assisted collectively; everyone has equal responsibility. Two schools, however, are special statistically—one above the system and one below the system. If the difference can be explained by neighborhood wealth, there is nothing to learn. However, often this is not the case and one school has insight to offer and one will need that insight.

Deming describes the two types of mistakes organizations can make. Both are costly. "Mistake 1: To react to an outcome as if it came from a special cause, when actually it came from common causes of variation. Mistake 2: To treat an outcome as if it came from common causes of variation, when actually it came from special causes."[16] The control chart can assist school district leaders as they attempt to avoid the two types of errors.

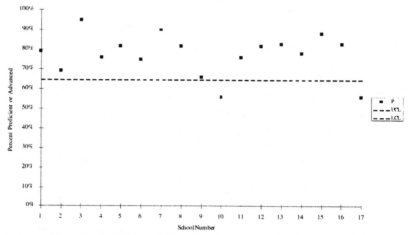

Figure 10.5. Grade 3 Control Chart for Seventeen Schools

Results Data Question 3

When school systems can answer yes to question 2, they are ready for question 3, "If yes, is there a culture of celebrating ATB's (all-time bests) by student, classroom, grade level, department, and school?

The American culture has a terrible habit of pulling numbers out of the air and making them goals for somebody else. Somebody somewhere says Christmas retail sales should increase by 5 percent. In January when the results are calculated, Christmas sales were 3.8 percent higher than ever before. However, the press is negative. The artificial goal was not met. Bad. Deming writes, "Anybody can achieve almost any goal by redefinition to terms, distortion and faking and running up costs."[17] At the time of this writing, significant debate is occurring regarding No Child Left Behind legislation. Read the newspapers—all three efforts are taking place simultaneously. I am not sure, but I believe if Congress had written NCLB to require constant improvement, the vast majority of educators would have embraced the challenge. When will the United States ever learn the harm caused by these artificial goals? Instead of people pulling numbers out of the air, we need to celebrate improvement, no matter how small. "Tremendous power exists in the fact of continued improvement and the delivery of results."[18]

One reason for the urgent need for these celebrations is that in our society "ninety-five per cent of changes made by management today make no improvement."[19] Teachers clearly know this, and students soon learn this. When a change does result in improvement, celebrations are needed. (It would be easy for readers to assume Deming was speaking of school administrators. No, he was speaking of all managers: industry, government, and education. When somebody says education should be more businesslike, one response is, "Education already is there; 95 percent of the changes do not result in improvement.")

A competition to determine the best school, the best teacher, the best student, or the best grade level will not create a superb school district. "With a competition, the second-place person—who may have missed by only a hair—is a loser. Competitions are typically all or none, which means many superb performers become losers. A team that is second or third (out of, say, eight) on every single criterion wins nothing, even though in a sense they may be the best overall performers of the year. Why not give each team an award for its most important accomplishment, or for its biggest improvement?"[20]

Results Data Question 4

If yes can be answered to the first three questions, then the district and its schools are ready for question 4, "Is there a record of increased achievement with a balanced curriculum?" This means that all subjects are taught at all grade levels. First graders have science, social studies, music, art, physical education, mathematics, writing, and reading. This is true for all grade levels. In other words, are the scales being tipped in favor of reading? "Did you win because you were smart or because you tipped the scales in your favor?" asks an article by Chip Heath and Dan Heath.[21] Some instructional programs generate impressive test results, but in the process they cannibalize the whole curriculum by offering students only reading and a little mathematics.

One very real problem in schools is pull-out. Out of which subject are students removed from the regular classroom for extra help in special education, Title I remedial, speech, or English Language Learning assistance? One system change that can be made is to assign all of these specialists to a different work day. They come to work two hours later and work two hours longer. Parents, in the IEP process, are given the choice of pull-out or after-school assistance. Of course, parents selecting the after-school choice must not rely on district transportation services. Some teachers will balk at such a suggestion, and others will gladly accept the change. The personnel department can change the schedule for the volunteers and only hire new teachers on the revised schedule.

Clearly, many instructional programs could have the same results by tipping the scales of time in their favor. The issue for educational leaders is to increase achievement levels *and* maintain a balanced curriculum with all subjects honored, including the arts and physical education. In fact, it could be argued that the very best schools *decrease* the amount of time allotted to reading each year and increase the time for literature, writing, and all other subjects. Why would this be true? It is because their teachers are so effective in teaching reading that kids read well and any additional time spent on reading subtracts from learning. I am not arguing here that schools should gradually decrease time for reading, but I am clearly stating that a top-notch school has impressive results in reading, writing, mathematics, *and* teaches all subjects in all grade levels. Tipping the scales today is taking action that produces even more mistakes tomorrow.[22]

NOTES

1. Deming, *The New Economics*, 25–27.
2. Ackoff, 36.
3. Reeves, 99.
4. Giuliani, *Leadership*, 310.
5. Freese, 56.
6. Giuliani, 96.
7. Reeves, 18.

8. Deming, *The New Economics*, 8.
9. Webber and Wallace, 10.
10. Schmoker, 34.
11. Webber and Wallace, 11.
12. Webber and Wallace, 18.
13. Kaplan and Norton, 17.
14. Liker, 255.
15. Webber and Wallace, 129.
16. Deming, *The New Economics*, 99.
17. Deming, *The New Economics*, 43.
18. Collins, 174.
19. Deming, *The New Economics*, 38.
20. Deci and Flaste, 155.
21. Chip Heath and Dan Heath, "Success Can Make You Stupid," *Fast Company* (May 2007): 70.
22. Deming, *The New Economics*, 39.

11

CURRICULUM

In order for the school board to be successful, the superintendent must be successful. In order for the school superintendent to be successful, the curriculum must be organized with the clear aim of removing permission to forget.

This chapter is not about what students should know and be able to do at the end of thirteen years of education. Many different subject and grade-level committees are necessary to describe the particulars of each content area, grade by grade and course by course. Within the allotted number of pages for this book, it cannot be written; the requirements are too vast.

This chapter is not about instruction, which is left for the next chapter. Further, there are countless other books that have the aim of improving teaching ability, instructional strategies, and classroom procedures.

This chapter is about the *structure* of the curriculum. How do school districts organize the curriculum so that all, or almost all, of the students meet the standards? Historically, school districts have relied upon textbook publishers to accomplish this. I do not know if publishers are up to the task or not. What I do observe, however, is that the textbook adoptions for school districts come from multiple publishers. The history/social science textbooks, for example, are purchased from multiple publishers over the thirteen-year K–12 experience. So if history/social science is unified and cohesive, it will be because the local educators made it unified and cohesive.

Curriculum Question 1

Are over 90 percent of the essential concepts students are to know and be able to do aligned within the school system from kindergarten through twelfth grade? Alignment, in order to have the power embedded in systems thinking, must be aligned within the school district from grade to grade and course to course. State standards are certainly a guide, but internal alignment is the key. People must know "how their work fits into the entire production system. With this knowledge workers can see how what they do affects others further down the production process."[1] Taking out the business language, educators must know what is taught in higher grades and what has been taught in prior grades. For example, the high-school geometry teachers must know what geometry is taught in each grade prior to high-school geometry. If the teachers do not have this knowledge on paper that can be distributed to students, much time is wasted in needless reteaching of prior content. Further, the students are able to pretend they were never taught any geometry in prior grade levels.

When a school district is fully aligned, then the following, at a minimum, will be in place:

A. Reading passages from each grade level, sample comprehension questions, and fluency rate expectations are agreed upon for each grade level.

B. Writing rubrics are in place for every grade level with agreed-upon samples at each level of the rubric. It must be obvious that the rubrics for each grade level are linked. Either the district has a 1–15 (or so) rubric describing kindergarten through twelfth-grade writing as one continuum or there is a set of cascading rubrics. For example, the 1–4 rubric for ninth grade is uploaded to tenth grade by dropping the lowest descriptor (level 1) and replacing it with a new descriptor at the highest level. The 1–4 rubric at tenth grade is really a ninth-grade 2–5 rubric renamed 1–4 for tenth grade. See table 11.1 for an elementary example.

Table 11.1. Sample Rubric

Kindergarten	Level 1 2 3 4 writing
First Grade	Level 2 3 4 5 writing
Second Grade	Level 3 4 5 6 writing
Third Grade	Level 4 5 6 7 writing

These levels can be re-numbered 1–4 for every grade level with the understanding that a scale of 1–4 in first grade is not the same as a 1–4 scale in any other grade level.

C. All editing (often labeled "daily oral language") expectations are established for each grade level. What errors are students expected to locate and correct at each grade level, 1 to 12?

D. All spelling words from kindergarten through eighth grade (or higher) are established.

E. All mathematics concepts, skills, and vocabulary are listed for grades K–8 and then for each high-school course. Sample problems to be solved are provided for each grade level and mathematics course.

F. All geography vocabulary and concepts are listed by grade level and course. All map/globe locations to be known by graduation are listed, beginning with the globe in kindergarten.

G. Major historical events to be understood are listed by grade level and course. The historical periods for each grade level are spelled out. Students, for example, are not repeating the same U.S. history course three times, but the three courses (fifth, eighth, and eleventh grade) are unique.

H. The science concepts, vocabulary, and processes to be known are written down for each grade level. If the same concept appears in a later grade level, it is clearly written exactly what is to be learned in more depth the second time around.

I. All other subjects have their vocabulary, concepts, principles, generalizations, and skills written down in progressive order.

All of this effort will cause some short-term pain and cost, but it will be worth it in the long run. The disjointed grade levels must be joined together to create a smooth flow from grade to grade and from elementary to middle to high school. Senge writes, "The fundamental characteristic of the relatively unaligned team is wasted energy. Individuals may work extraordinarily hard, but their efforts do not efficiently translate to team effort. By contrast, when a team becomes more aligned, a commonality of direction emerges, and individuals' energies harmonize.There is less wasted energy. In fact, a resonance or synergy develops, like the coherent light of a laser rather than the incoherent and scatter light of a light bulb."[2] Education clearly has many, many people who work extraordinarily hard with wasted efforts. Sad. He further writes, "Individuals do not sacrifice their personal interests to the larger team vision; rather, the shared vision becomes an extension of their personal visions. In fact, alignment is the *necessary condition* before empowering the individual will empower the whole team. Empowering the individual when there is relatively low level of alignment worsens the chaos."[3]

Curriculum Question 2

Question 2: Are the students and parents provided the aligned curriculum documents? Are parents and students provided the learning objectives for the current grade level or course, at least one future course, and at least two prior grade levels or courses?

This is not accomplished by providing a copy of state standards. By the very nature of state standards, they are general. For example, a reasonable state standard for intermediate grades is "To know major geographical locations in the western hemisphere." The district documents provided to parents and students provide the exact locations to be known at the end of each year.

A school district meeting this communication requirement provides kindergarten or first-grade parents example stories from every grade level from kindergarten through at least fifth grade. The parents have example comprehension questions for each story (ideally the questions are 50 percent about the story just read and 50 percent asking students to compare and contrast this story with prior readings). Further, parents and students are provided the words per minute students would be expected to read for each grade level's passage.

Curriculum Question 3

Curriculum question 3: Are students given a common end-of-grade level/course exam? Are all parents notified of their student's performance on this assessment? This need not always be a written exam, but it must be commonly administered throughout the district. For example, it matters not if Algebra I is taken at the middle school, the ninth-grade center, the comprehensive high school, or the continuation high school. All students are administered the same final.

Regarding these assessments, it is perfectly appropriate to give students choices. The exam can instruct students to select two essay questions, each counting for 50 percent of the grade, or to select one essay and a set of problems/open-ended questions, and so on. The common assessment agreement can contain student choices in demonstrating knowledge.[4]

Thompson writes, "I do not teach anything—especially a book—as a self-contained unit. I am convinced that as soon as students perceive a unit to have concluded, they discard its intellectual contents. In fact students will ask you: Do we have to know this for the test? What they are asking for is permission to forget. If you tell them the first novel will not be included on the second novel's test, you're telling them it's over. When it's over for the teacher, it's over for the kids."[5]

Thompson has described the control the teachers have over their classroom system. Teachers do not need to give permission to forget from chapter to chapter, unit to unit, or spelling test to spelling test. In order for a school system to answer yes to curriculum question 4, permission to forget must be removed from the school district.

Curriculum Question 4

Curriculum question 4: "Has a structure and ratio been established to remove 'permission to forget' from prior grade levels and courses?" Does the end-of-the-year assessment include an agreed-upon percentage of questions from prior grade levels and courses? Often the percentage selected is 70 percent from the current course and 30 percent from the prior courses. For example, the eleventh-grade U.S. history final could be 70 percent eleventh-grade history (1900 to current time), and 30 percent prior U.S. history, taught in fifth grade and eighth grade. Algebra II finals could be 70 percent Algebra II, 10 percent Algebra I, 10 percent geometry, and 10 percent middle-school general math.

When a district has over 90 percent of its curriculum internally aligned, parents and students are informed at the beginning of each year precisely what is to be learned, the end-of-the-year assessments are common throughout the district, and students do not have permission to forget from year to year, then the district has a curriculum structure in place that only needs to be updated from time to time.

Further, students will be much more internally motivated with such a structure. Think about it: Four years of students' life in schools is review. Boring. "Providing others with challenges that will allow them to end up feeling both competent and autonomous, will promote in them greater vitality, motivation, and well-being."[6]

Schmoker has written about this issue from a different vantage point, which is the pressure to increase the school day and the school year.[7] Since teachers tell me that they spend, on the average, 60 days a year reviewing prior years' content (at a cost of over $100 billion per year), taking away "permission to forget" can capture more days for learning than state legislatures could ever afford.[8]

NOTES

1. Webber and Wallace, 36.
2. Senge, 234.
3. Senge, 234–35.
4. Thompson, 68.
5. Thompson, 62.
6. Deci and Flaste, 70.
7. Schmoker, 90.
8. Jenkins, 144.

12

INSTRUCTION

In order for the school board to be successful, the superintendent must be successful. In order for the school superintendent to be successful, student learning must not depend upon which students are assigned to which teachers.

Instruction Question 1

The first instructional question is, "Are standards the foundation for instruction?" Teachers are provided textbooks, other books, and/or other resource materials. They also have access to state standards for their particular subject(s). The school district provides a scope and sequence of learning objectives or some other form of a curriculum/standards guide. Anybody who looks at the instructional textbooks and the standards sees a disconnect. Why? So far, the major U.S. publishers have not figured out how to match materials to each of the different state standards. To exacerbate the situation further, the textbooks are not written K–12. Some publishers specialize in elementary and others in secondary. School districts often have textbooks from three to four different publishers for one K–12 academic discipline. To expect each teacher to study the state standards, the district curriculum guides, and then select the specific chapters that met both district and state guidelines *and* create new materials for the standards that are not taught in the textbook is living in a fantasy world. It is not going to happen. Schmoker writes, "What do we see in the vast majority of classrooms? We find startling amounts of busy work, with no connection to important standards or a common curriculum . . . In most cases, neither teachers nor students can articulate what they are supposed to be learning that day . . . For the majority of lessons, no evidence exists by which a teacher could gauge or report on how well students are learning the essential standards."[1] However, districts that can answer yes to instruction question 1 have organized themselves so that teachers have appropriate materials for each standard, teachers know which textbook chapters are superfluous, and teachers know which materials to use to meet standards not covered by the textbook.

Further, when students are not meeting the learning expectations, these school districts analyze which standards are the most difficult and proceed to remedy that portion of the instructional program. The school district that cannot answer yes to instructional question 1 is almost always program-based, not standards-based. When questioned regarding why a particular topic is taught, the response is that it is the next chapter rather than that students at a grade level are expected to know and apply this content. Sometimes the answer is the district purchases this expensive computer-based program and we are required to take the students down to the computer lab thirty minutes each day. There is nothing in the answer that implies standards are the foundation for the instruction.

If enough problems surface, these districts decide to throw out the current program and start over with a new one. Sometimes they make an even worse decision; they keep the old program and mandate another add-on program. Since these districts are unable to lengthen the school day, they subtract time from nontested academic subjects to meet the needs of tested subjects.

When teachers meet with their principal to discuss student learning, is the discussion about being sure to use a particular commercial program? Or is the discussion about which standards seem to be the most difficult for the students? When principals meet with their supervisors, is the discussion about a particular program or about students meeting standards? A yes to question 1 means the total focus is upon meeting standards, not about using a particular strategy, leased software, or textbook. It is never, at nine weeks, "Have the teachers 'covered' 25 percent of the book?", but "Have the students met 25 percent of the end-of-the-year standards?"

When a district is standards-based, alternative strategies are not only possible, but encouraged. "Rolls-Royce and Toyota are both known for the high quality of their cars, yet the processes they use to produce their products couldn't be more different . . . Following quality standards doesn't mean that you have to do everything the same way as everyone else; it simply means that your customers get what they expect when they buy your product or service."[2]

One way for districts to assess if they are standards-based or not is to question teachers about their grade distribution. Guskey and Bailey write eloquently on this topic. "When challenged on the grades they assign or accused of grade inflation, teachers need only point to the standards or goals used in determining the grades. So long as those standards are sufficiently rigorous and appropriate for that grade level of course, the assigned marks or grades can be easily defended."[3] All teachers should be able to defend poor grades or a high percentage of As with the same examination of learning standards. Did the students learn what was expected?

Instruction Question 2

Question 2 is, "Have district staff agreed upon the ingredients of powerful instruction? Do classroom observations document that these practices are in place over 90 percent of the time?"

Have the district staff members agreed upon the ingredients of powerful instruction to be included in all units? Are there structures in place for every grade level to build background knowledge through novels, field trips, video, guest speakers, school environment, technology, and direct vocabulary instruction? What is to be included in a perfect unit? How is background knowledge taught? What about Bloom's taxonomy? Consider deeper and deeper content, moving from facts to concepts to principles to generalizations. It is not that school districts expect all units to be perfect. Are all board meetings perfect? Of course not, and neither will be all units. Nevertheless, having a description of perfect will greatly assist learning and teaching. We probably cannot even afford perfect—take field trips, for example. On the other hand, many elementary schools are within walking distance of the local high school and there are superb field trips for elementary students at the high school. For example, I heard rave reviews when each physics student explained the science that interested five-year-olds to a kindergarten student.

In his book *Classics in the Classroom*, Thompson lists categories of thinking and feeling that need to be considered in a district's description of the ideal unit. Thompson does not arrange them in any sort of "hierarchy of complexity or importance."[4] Readers must not forget the title of his book, look at the list, and wonder where reading, writing, and debate are. They are everywhere.

Memory: Recall
Cognition: Comprehension
Reason: Avoiding logical errors
Synthesis: Combining or connecting ideas
Divergence: Thinking of alternatives
Convergence: Choosing one idea
Evaluation: Deciding value by criteria
Ethics: Deciding moral value
Analysis: Studying components
Application: Using ideas
Intuition: Ideas from the blue
Imagination: Seeing mental images
Emotion: Feelings
Aesthetics: Artistic/sensory feelings
Disassumption: Escaping false assumptions

Because I have spent so much of my career teaching with mathematics manipulatives, I cannot go further without elaborating upon "seeing mental images." The purpose of mathematics manipulatives is to create mental images. People who have not used them think the manipulatives are a crutch necessary for the very young or the very slow. In fact, all students need help creating mental images. "Bucky's [Buckminster Fuller is best known for the geodesic dome, but patented many other inventions] love of geometry, in particular, began with his kindergarten exposure to the construction tools of dried peas and toothpicks."[5]

"Instead of overwhelming folks with reams of minutiae and too-rigid instructions, [the policy book of Starbucks] gives guiding principles of the environments [management] hopes to create and legendary service they strive to provide. This is leadership at its best: simple instruction provided in an appealing way, with a spirit that offers hope."[6] If Starbucks can figure out how to provide their employees guidance without demeaning them, certainly school districts can accomplish the same.

The ingredients for a powerful unit must include time for reflection. Often, students remember the reflection activity more than the actual instruction. When brainstorming reflection ideas, ask the question, "How do human beings tell their stories?" The answer is writing, song, dance, drama, and art. No matter what the subject, a small amount of time for reflection will enhance both the students' joy and their memory.

The commercial pictures above the alphabet in elementary classrooms should be removed; it is the students' job to create the art. For example, the teacher has concluded reading a novel to the students and now the students are agreeing on pictures and labels for each letter of the alphabet. "What is a good label for A, for B, for C, and so on to help us remember aspects of the novel?" Each student contributes a picture and label for one letter. This simple reflection concept can be expanded into ABC books written by whole classes or individuals to reflect upon their learning of content standards. I've seen the *ABC Book of Canada*, the *ABC Book of Mathematics* (j for adjacent), the *ABC Book of Ancient Egypt* (*x* for sphinx), and even the *ABC Book of Welding* with very technical writing and illustrations.

The two examples above involve both art and writing; other reflection activities will utilize music, drama, speech, the making of games, and clever uses of technology. The point is that districts have agreed upon the components of powerful instruction and have included reflection as one component.

A combination of question 1 and question 2 can be visualized as a matching exercise. Column one is standards, and column two lists ingredients of powerful instruction. During planning time, teachers match standards to instructional strategies. They also discover which strategies best meet the needs of their students.

It is not that school systems want every teacher employing the same exact teaching processes, but that agreement must be reached upon the ingredients of powerful instruction. If these ingredients are not agreed upon, the school district is likely to become a victim of programs of the month and a very unstable system.

Instruction Question 3

Question 3 is, "Are all teachers members of at least one group of peers meeting regularly to study student learning, to agree upon pacing guides, to study item analyses, and to review teaching strategies?" "What schools most need now: to begin systematically harnessing the power of collective intelligence that already resides in the school to solve problems."[7] DuFour and others write further, "Although individual growth is essential for organizational growth to take place, it does not guarantee organizational growth. Building a school's capacity to learn is a collective rather than an individual task. People who engage in collaborative team learning are able to learn from one another and thus create momentum to fuel continued improvement. It is difficult to overstate the importance of collaborative teams in the improvement process."[8]

Along the same lines, Ackoff writes, "Once planners and managers give up the idea of redesigning the work of others and, instead, give them an opportunity to design their own work and work environment, they have no difficulty in bringing about changes that lead to significant improvements in their quality of work life."[9]

Senge's insights about learning teams are helpful. I have included several that seemed most helpful to educators as they continue their efforts in developing learning communities. He writes, "The purpose of dialog is to go beyond any one individual's understanding. We are not trying to win in a dialog. We all win if we are doing it right. In dialog, individuals gain insights that simply could not be achieved individually."[10] "Contrary to popular myth, great teams are not characterized by an absence of conflict . . . In great teams conflict becomes productive."[11] "Defensive routines can become a surprising ally toward building a learning team by providing a signal when learning is not occurring . . . If you think about it, one of the most useful skills of a learning team would be the ability to recognize when people are not reflecting on their own assumptions, when they are not inquiring into each other's thinking, when they are not exposing their thinking in a way that encourages others to inquire into it."[12] "Learning teams practice a special form of alchemy, the transformation of potentially divisive conflict and defensiveness into learning."[13] "If anything, team skills are more challenging to develop than individual skills."[14]

Teachers need an annual pacing plan just like the business offices need a budget. Financial officers have dollars, and teachers have time. The budget and the end-of-the-year financial statements never match 100 percent, and the teachers' pacing guides will not match the actual teaching sequence 100 percent. Nevertheless, the pacing plan is a key component of appropriate instruction keeping "us focused throughout the year."[15] The school district can greatly assist this planning process by providing teachers three-column paper. The left column lists standards, the middle column the expected week number for the teaching of each standard, and the third column is for notes on resource materials. The goal is not for somebody else to write the pacing guide and hand it to the teachers. It is the teachers' job, in committees of like teachers, to write the pacing guide.

In my seminars I ask, "What percentage of the year do you spend teaching content students should already know prior to coming into your classroom?" The predominant answer is one-third of the year. Thus, if permission to forget is not removed from the district through its curriculum structure, then teachers will start their pacing guide on week thirteen. All they need to write in weeks one through twelve is review of prior years. Eleventh-grade U.S. history teachers might write for week one "review of elementary U.S. history (up through American Revolution)"; week 2, "review of middle-school U.S. history (constitution to 1900)"; and then begin the pacing for their high-school standards in week three. In the third column, it is helpful to teachers if the curriculum staff lists textbook chapters, videos, URLs, and so on to assist with standards-based instruction.

The ideal pacing guides would not only include the standards for the current grade level or course but also the standards for the prior two years/courses and the next two years/courses. The instructional responsibility is to introduce two years early and to apply at higher levels of cognition content taught one to two years prior. For example, in mathematics the responsibility is to, with manipulatives, introduce content two years early, make sure students can function abstractly with current grade-level standards, and challenge students with provocative problem-solving using concepts taught the prior two years. The instruction on the prior two years is not traditional review, but application, synthesis, and analysis of key standards from prior years. In history, "introduce" may be reading a historical fiction novel set in the time period students will study next year. The reinforcement of prior history most often gives students a deeper understanding of prior years' standards.

A district that can answer yes to instructional question 3 has a format for teachers to plan their individual pacing guides and an expectation that they will be used and adjusted throughout the school year. The adjustments and notes they make will be the starting point for next year's pacing guide. "Some leaders make the mistake of delegating the responsibility but failing to delegate authority and power to actually accomplish what's being required. Don't simply give orders, but rather give freedom for people to carry out the instructions."[16] Teachers in a learning community can write their own pacing guides. As I write this, I can hear push back from some administrators. They are thinking that they must provide the pacing guide for the teachers and inspect the teachers to be sure they are on target. Otherwise, some students will not be taught some content and big holes will be present in students' learning. This is a good time to visit Dr. Deming's four generations of management: (1) I just do it myself, (2) do it the way I tell you, (3) management by objective, and (4) agreement upon a common aim and working together to accomplish the aim.

Generation one is impossible; principals know they cannot teach all of the students. Generation two is providing a pacing guide to all teachers and monitoring their progress. While it is better than the principal attempting to teach 500 students, it is not the best. Generation three would be each teacher selecting the standards they like and writing their own pacing guide with their favorite standards. If the students meet the standards the teacher selected, the teacher is fine. Generation four is a district where there is agreement upon the standards, upon the locations of the materials for teaching the standards, and even collaboration among teachers teaching the same course as they write their pacing guides. The principal may be a part of the planning team.

Item analysis by grade level or department is powerful. Teachers who meet in teams, often labeled professional learning communities, must spend a portion of their time analyzing student errors and making plans to reduce the errors. For example:

1. A school has five teachers at a particular grade level and all assign a paper with the same writing prompt.
2. The papers are gathered from all five classes.
3. Five papers are randomly selected for each teacher to tally errors.
4. The teachers each tally the errors for their five papers.
5. The total errors from the twenty-five papers are tabulated.
6. The team of five teachers uses the data to prepare for future instruction.

A key component of this process is that teachers are looking at papers from multiple classrooms. The random sampling provides accurate data in minimum time, and the collaboration between teachers provides accurate analysis. Reeves wrote, "A teacher should exchange student work with a colleague for review and collaborative evaluation at least once every two weeks. Collaboration is the hallmark of effective implementation of standards."[17] Without the random sampling of five papers from each room, the superb Reeves advice seems overwhelming. How can a teacher inspect 100 percent of his/her own papers and then inspect somebody else's papers? They can, in less time than 100 percent inspection, with random sampling. One Arizona school agreed to use this random process seven of each nine weeks. The other two weeks, teachers would not meet because the time would be used to grade 100 percent of the papers for the upcoming report card.

The exact same procedure can be used for any subject in any grade level where there are multiple staff teaching the same content. Hopefully, the discussion is about long-term learning as described in chapter 9 and not about short-term memory as measured by traditional spelling tests and chapter tests. I would never suggest that teachers waste their valuable time conferring over student short-term memory assignments.

Of course, some of the planning time together is to share successes and failures with particular teaching strategies. The components of powerful instruction can be an outline for this conversation. One final note on teams: Maybe a small budget would help. "Each team has a budget of $200 to be spent at its discretion,"[18] is a portion of team direction in the book *Fish!* The authors also expect teams to report back to all employees on team progress.

Instruction Question 4

Instruction question 4 has two parts: (1) has the school district identified all of the activities that are necessary only because of some instructional failure and (2) is there a district-created flowchart designed to reduce these failures? The steps for identifying the cost of failure are outlined by Webber and Wallace.[19] Step one is to "identify all activities that are necessary only because of poor quality." In education they are summer school; students in special education only because of reading problems, sixty days each fall in most classrooms assigned to review prior years' content, adding a year of education for a pupil because of retention; reteaching any class because of failing grades; Title I; cost of GEDs; and a high percentage of counselors' time and all administrative time spent on a failure of students to behave properly.

Step two from Webber and Wallace is "Determine where in the production process these activities occur." This involves asking why at least five times to determine the root cause of the issue. In education, we are tempted to go back to a root cause of poor legislation or poor parenting. We cannot solve legislative and societal problems. We must stop our five whys with what we can influence as educators.

For each failure, administrators must track the source, find the biggest causes of this failure, and attack the issue with vengeance. An example of high cost of failure is Fs in high school. The first task is counting, by course, the number of failing grades. Then come the five whys. Why, why, why, why, and why do we have this issue? Persist with the determination of a three-year-old questioning why something works as it does. Sometimes the reason for the high failure rate is teachers who strongly believe they must be accountable for teaching both content and responsibility. The teachers are in a situation where the report card does not have a course called responsibility, so their only choice is to include responsibility as a component of the content grade. In order to stop the failure hemorrhage, teachers must either (1) stop failing students for lack of responsibility, (2) agree that students are responsible for learning and not responsible for teaching methods (homework is a method, not a subject), or (3) the administrators must add responsibility to the report card as a subject. All teachers submit a responsibility grade into the grading software. All responsibility grades are averaged from various teachers for the final responsibility grade on the report card.

Readers must not assume that I believe homework is bad. Just like movies, some homework is bad and some is good. Further, I am addressing daily homework and not long-term projects. Curriculum has two aspects: what students know and what they can do. In general, daily homework's purpose is practice remembering the "know" aspect of curriculum. The long-term assignments generally are the application of the "can do" curriculum component. Most long-term assignments are for the purpose of deeper understanding and application. The evaluation is designed to determine if students learned. Thus readers should not mix up my thoughts on daily homework and long-term, deeper understanding assignments, which are usually very important.

If schools agree on choice two above, which means that responsibility is defined as being responsible for the learning, then some suggestions I've learned from two teachers may be of interest to readers. First, John MacDonald of Mayo High School in Rochester, Minnesota, provides this plan for daily homework. He assigns homework but does not grade or collect it. Each time students have an assignment, either in class or out of class, they know they will have a two- to six-item graded quiz from the assignment. The questions will be worded exactly as on the assignment. This solves several problems: (1) students understand they are responsible for learning the content, (2) good students are not punished by having to practice something they already know, (3) no more credit is given for copied homework, and (4) teacher preparation is given a higher priority than student grading. I suggest that teachers stay with their same percentage for homework they have now. Further, they tell the students they can earn a certain number of homework points over the grading period. This number equals the number of questions they'll be asked over the course of the grading period—maybe two questions today, three the next day, and so on, but students know the total for the grading period.

Woody Wilson of Parkersburg High School in Parkersburg, West Virginia, has a unique structure for the performance-based assignments. First, students are told what they are expected to learn from the assignment. Then he provides three choices. Students can prove they met the learning standard by completing one of three assignments. Further, he lists a "?," which means if a student has another idea how they can learn the required material, he or she can propose it to the teacher.

Some school staff members have agreed on a form that students may fill out when requesting permission for an interdisciplinary assignment. The students are requesting permission to complete one larger project instead of two or three smaller ones. Teachers sign off ahead of time and agree upon a due date.

All three high-school examples are provided to assist administrators and teachers with one cause of failure in schools: students being graded on homework policies and not on meeting learning standards. Douglas Reeves wrote, "Standards do endure not through legislative mandates or administrative cheerleading, but because they are the fairest way to assess student performance."[20] Homework policy is clearly not the only cause of failure but is a contributing factor. Each root cause of failure must be researched, with alternatives given to teachers so that the failure rate can be reduced year after year.

Step three from Webber and Wallace asks us to "identify the percentage of effort that each corrective activity consumes in its part of the production process." For education, it is the percentage of Summer school caused by failure, the percentage of special education that is merely a reading problem, the percentage of counselor time spent dealing with failing students, the percentage of administrator time spent dealing with failing students, and the percentage of teacher time spent reteaching a previously failed course.

Step four from Webber and Wallace is a sobering task: "Sum the cost of poor quality for each area to get the total for your organization." "Frontline employees must understand the financial consequences of their decisions and actions; senior executives must understand the drivers of long-term financial success."[21] There are full-time teachers in some larger high schools that their only students are ones that have previously flunked the course they are teaching. Think how many more music, art, and career-tech courses we could offer if students learned the content the first time around.

Educators must calculate the dollar cost for failure and then divide by students to create cost per student. Could it be that $3,000 or more per student per year is spent on dealing with failure?

What now? A school district that can answer yes to question 4 not only has identified all activities that are necessary because of poor quality but it has also an agreed-upon flowchart for teachers and administrators to follow when there is a learning difficulty. "The first step in any organization is to draw a flow diagram to show how each component depends on others. Then everyone may understand what his job is. If people do not see the process, they can not improve it."[22] Poor quality and failure will not go away, but the percentage of time spent on rework and the total cost of rework can go down greatly. It is not that educators are driven by saving costs. However, they do want to spend the money on added value for students instead of rework. More arts, more field trips, more technology, more books, more career-tech, and more time for administrators to be in the classroom instead of punishing students is the driving force.

DuFour et al. write,

"1. What is it we want all students to learn—by grade level, by course, and by unit of instruction?
2. How will we know when each student has acquired the intended knowledge and skills?
3. How will we respond when students experience initial difficulty so that we can improve upon current levels of learning?"[23]

In this book, I have written about questions one and two in the curriculum and process data chapters. Their question three is the focus of the rest of this chapter.

I suggest the first question in the flowchart be, "Is this a reading problem? If no, proceed to another page to identify the difficulty. If yes, proceed to further reading questions." The next question can be, "Is this a beginning reading problem?" If no, the staff members are directed to questions regarding comprehension. If yes, the next question could be, "Have all three approaches to reading been attempted?" The three approaches are sound, word (as in *Dick and*

Jane), and sentence (using music, art, literature, and student-generated writing). If the answer is no, direct the educators to resource materials for all three approaches. If the answer is yes, direct educators to further questions regarding memory, behavior, psychology, and so on. By the time the flowchart is completed, all of the expertise of the district and beyond will be utilized. Clearly, vision and hearing problems have to be addressed in the flowchart.

Somewhere in the flowchart will be a series of other questions:

1. Does the student have an all-encompassing interest?
2. Are we sure this is a reading problem and not a compliance problem?
3. Does the student have prior learning successes that can be connected to solve the current problem?
4. Is it memory? Has Reuven Feuerstein's Mediated Learning Experience (MLE) been explored?
5. Has the student been retained in prior grades and has never accepted the retention, and should the district consider returning the student to his/her age-appropriate grade level?
6. Is the intervention school- and districtwide rather than left up to each teacher?
7. Is the intervention timely?[24]
8. Is the intervention directive?[25] In other words, can the student opt out of the intervention? Is the district offering learning opportunities or establishing structures for all to learn?

A district that can answer yes to instructional question 4 uses this flowchart when problems occur. Without such a plan, students who struggle are subjected to a "de facto educational lottery program."[26] Their success depends upon the luck of classroom assignments. If many of the structures described in this book are not in place, the flowchart will overwhelm the district. However, once a great deal of systemic action has occurred over a number of years, the flowchart will have significant value in the toughest of cases. "Quality assurance is more than just checking to see that the product or service meets the customers' expectations; you also have to look at the process involved in creating the product or service to see if you're capable of producing a quality product or service each and every time."[27]

NOTES

1. Schmoker, 15–16.
2. Webber and Wallace, 27.
3. Guskey and Bailey, 137.
4. Thompson, 49–57.
5. Sieden, 25.
6. Michelli, 21.
7. DuFour, DuFour, Eaker, and Kaharnek, xiii.
8. DuFour, DuFour, Eaker, and Kaharnek, 3.
9. Ackoff, 77.
10. Senge, 241.
11. Senge, 249.
12. Senge, 256.
13. Senge, 257.
14. Senge, 258.
15. Patricia Davenport and Gerald Anderson, *Closing the Achievement Gap* (Houston, TX: American Productivity and Quality Center, 2002), 73.
16. Huckabee, 183.
17. Reeves, 67.
18. Stephen C. Lundin, Harry Paul, and John Christensen, *Fish!* (New York: Hyperion, 2000), 85.
19. Webber and Wallace, 21.
20. Reeves, 7.
21. Kaplan and Norton, 8.
22. Deming, 29–30.
23. DuFour, DuFour, Eaker, and Kaharnek, 2–3.
24. DuFour, DuFour, Eaker, and Kaharnek, 7.
25. DuFour, DuFour, Eaker, and Kaharnek, 8.
26. DuFour, DuFour, Eaker, and Kaharnek, 33.
27. Webber and Wallace, 34.

CHARTING YOUR PROGRESS

The dodecagon entitled "Charting Your Progress" is provided for readers to shade in their assessment of their school district (division in Canada). Readers are encouraged to shade in their baseline data in one color and then each year add additional colors to show progress over time.

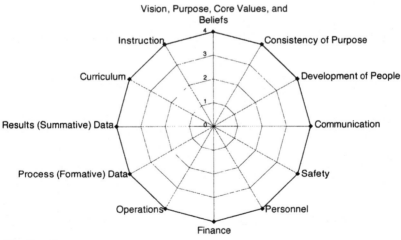

Charting Progress

AFTERWORD

"That an author might disagree with Shewhart's point of view made no difference to Shewhart, so long as a book would stimulate people to think."[1] In chapter 12, I wrote about the three most essential components for learning. These are the components leaders should observe the vast majority of the time when they visit classrooms. They are reading, writing, and activities that provoke deep thought. First of all, because you are reading this book, reading is taking place. I hope that you are taking notes, writing in the margins, and completing the provided dodecagon for tracking progress. Most of all, I hope you, the reader, are pondering the thoughts in this book.

As a former school superintendent, I learned that whatever committee I was working with was able to make better decisions in less time if I presented a rough draft. The group then went to work tearing apart the document, revising, scratching out, and eventually ending up with a document the group owned. I do not pretend that all readers will agree with the 48 questions I have written in the twelve categories. Some may not even believe I have the categories right. However, it is my hope that because of the process of rejecting what I have written readers will replace the questions with ones that make sense for their particular school district or division.

Once the 48 questions are agreed upon in a district or division, they are to be used not only to communicate the direction of the organization but also be used to manage strategy. In business, Kaplan and Norton found, "Within a year after starting the scorecard effort, each organization was using the scorecard as the cornerstone of its management system."[2]

When directors or superintendents meet with their colleagues, the pressure is to use 100 percent of the time for issues at hand. Between the legislature, school board, employee concerns, and parent issues, there can be no time for systemic, long-term discussion, reflection, and action. I recommend that the quarterly meetings be given over 100 percent to systemic action with reports on accomplishments and plans. It is not too much to ask that four times a year key leaders spend no time on the urgent.

For each of the twelve categories, one person is responsible for the strategic action. In larger districts and divisions, this person will have direct reports who can implement one aspect of the strategic action. The superintendent or director should then give the person responsible for the action a reporting time line. Choices are

1. in person every week
2. an e-mail every week
3. in person every month
4. an e-mail every month
5. in person every quarter

Further, I recommend that no matter which of the five are chosen that an additional e-mail be required each quarter of each person with direct responsibility for the strategic action. These e-mails are posted on the district's server prior to the quarterly strategic action meeting so all can read everyone else's report. The password-accessed documents are set up so that other key leaders can respond to their colleagues' work. Because education has so long been plagued by silos, this cross-departmental communication will do much to assist a district or division in achieving its vision.

One of the key advantages of the strategic action questions and dodecagon recording sheet is communication with the board of education. The boards need assistance in visualizing all that needs to be addressed in a school system, and the key administrators need help communicating all that is to be accomplished. Also, many times school board members have a longer tenure than several superintendents. The recording of progress on the dodecagon communicates progress to a new superintendent and assists the board in keeping a consistent focus in spite of changed leadership.

Another key advantage of the strategic action questions and dodecagon recording sheet is discouraging suboptimization. When organizations suboptimize, some departments win at the expense of the whole system. This would occur when the personnel office is so determined to staff every school with superb teachers that it hires only proven, experienced teachers. Personnel wins; finance loses. (My direction to principals and the personnel office was to only hire veteran, proven teachers who were near the top of the salary schedule, when the new hire could solve a big problem for us.) On the other hand, if the finance office says only hire first-year teachers, finance wins and instruction loses. The system is suboptimized in the other direction.

Principals often have difficulty keeping up with the thoughts of those in the central office. Their focus, as it should be, is on their school. When the leaders speak of their vision for instruction for several months and then seem to switch to a focus upon personnel practices, it looks like a pendulum with an ever-changing focus. However, with the twelve aspects of the dodecagon before all leaders on a consistent basis, all can see the vision of the school system and more easily change conversation from one of the twelve to another strand.

Educators can learn from business executives and their experience with the balanced scorecard. The barriers they list are

"1. Visions and strategies are not actionable

2. Strategies that are not linked to departmental, team, and individual goals

3. Strategies that are not linked to long- and short-term resource allocation

4. Feedback that is tactical, not strategic"[3]

When I have sat with school administrators looking over their strategic plans, the observation often is that either the plan is not worth implementing or there is no way to know if it was ever achieved as the platitudes are really mumbo jumbo. Further, the strategies seem to be left in the lap of the superintendents, and nobody else has any responsibility. Then there's the budget allocation process, which has no connection to the strategic plan. Finally, the feedback that comes to the superintendents is about the day-to-day short-term and not about the systemic plan. The quarterly strategic action meeting is designed to overcome this barrier.

NOTES

1. Cecelia S. Kilian, *The World of W. Edwards Deming* (Knoxville, TN: SPC Press, 1992), 93.
2. Kaplan and Norton, 275.
3. Kaplan and Norton, 193.

THE 48-ITEM FINAL

Graded exams are structured in several ways, none of which are from a systems perspective. They are given as if each teacher is an island unto him or herself, not as if the teacher is a part of a thirteen-year system, K–12. Sometimes teachers give chapter tests. Students know that when the chapter is over, they have permission to forget the chapter content. In many, many districts large expenditures have been made to give students quarterly exams. These are being marketed as formative assessments when they are really summative more often. Because the second-quarter exam asks no questions about first-quarter content, again students soon learn they have permission to forget prior quarters. Each quarter is an entity unto itself, just like each teacher can be a separate entity.

In some places, students have end-of-the-year graded finals. The rules here are that students are expected to remember the content for a whole year before forgetting it. Many states have a graduation exam. No matter what the grades are, students must also pass this exam. Essentially, this is unfair. The school system does not have in place a structure requiring students to remember, but places the whole burden on the student. The state-imposed exam would be a no-brainer if permission to forget was removed from the school system.

Below are two examples of a systems approach to creating finals. The first is for a first-year course with no prior knowledge required. This example works perfectly for first-year Spanish, as there is no prerequisite knowledge. The second example is for most courses where students should be required to remember prior content. An example is eleventh-grade U.S. history. Students are provided a list of key concepts for fifth-grade history and eighth-grade history and now they are in eleventh grade. The teacher expects students to remember prior history and is holding them accountable. It is reasonable to spend one week reviewing history taught in fifth grade (European exploration to the American Revolution) and one week reviewing eighth-grade history (1800s) and then spend the rest of the year on eleventh-grade history (1900 to current time). Students can see that one-third of their grade is fifth-grade and eighth-grade history. In chapter 9 and in my book *Improving Student Learning*, I describe classroom process data that prepares students for having to remember. In each example, students are provided four different end-of-the-year finals. The first is given at nine weeks, the second at semester, the third at third quarter, and the fourth at the final at the end of the year. Students like knowing what is to be expected at the end of the year and believe the grading scale below is fair.

Ideally, grades should correlate perfectly with learning. One should be able to believe, with great confidence, that a student receiving an A in a classroom has placed the content of the course into his or her long-term memory and can apply the knowledge in new situations as demonstrated by performance assignments. The student may or may not be particularly responsible when it comes to daily assignments. This information can be communicated to parents in ways other than academic grades.

OPTION 1: COURSE WITH NO
PREREQUISITE KNOWLEDGE

Students are given a minimum of four end-of-the-year finals. Each assessment is a different version, but all are based upon the course

Table A1

Time of Exam	Expectation	Grading Scale
First Quarter	25%—12 of 48	11 = A; 10 = B; 9 = C; 8 = D
Semester	25%—12 of 48	22 = A; 20 = B; 18 = C; 16 = D
Third Quarter	75%—36 of 48	33 = A; 30 = B; 27 = C; 24 = D
End of Course	100%—48 of 48	44 = A; 40 = B; 36 = C; 32 = D

expectations provided to students the first week of class. Students are expected to answer the percentage of the exam questions that correspond to the percentage of the course taught. For example, at the end of the first quarter, students are expected to answer 25 percent of the questions correctly. A grading scale for an exam with 48 questions could look like this if 90 percent equals an A and so on.

OPTION 2: COURSE REQUIRING PREREQUISITE KNOWLEDGE

Students are informed that one-third of their grade on exams will be their knowledge of prior grade/course content and two-thirds their knowledge of the current course. They are no longer given permission to forget the work of prior years. Students are provided, if necessary, the content expectations of prior courses. The grading scale combines the expectation of knowing 100 percent of prior-year content and the appropriate percentage of current year content. The example below is for an exam with 48 questions.

Table A2

Time of Exam	Prior Expectation	Current Expectation	Grading Scale
First Quarter	100%—16 questions	25%—8 of 32	22 = A; 19 = B; 17 = C; 14 = D
Semester	100%—16 questions	50%—16 of 32	29 = A; 26 = B; 22 = C; 19 = D
Third Quarter	100%—16 questions	75%—24 of 32	36 = A; 32 = B; 28 = C; 24 = D
End of Course	100%—16 questions	100%—32 of 32	43 = A; 38 = B; 34 = C; 29

THE 48 QUESTIONS

FROM SYSTEMS THINKING TO SYSTEMIC ACTION: 48 KEY QUESTIONS TO GUIDE THE JOURNEY

"The bottom line of systems thinking is leverage—seeing where the actions and changes to structures can lead to significant, enduring improvements. Often leverage follows the principle of economy of means: where the best results come not from large-scale efforts but from small well-focused actions."[1]

"The principal difference between excellent and ordinary organizational diagnosticians does not lie in the differences in the diagnoses they infer from the same information, but in the questions they ask to obtain additional relevant information. The information they obtain through their additional questions reduces the probability of an incorrect diagnosis."[2]

The Overall System

I.   Vision, Purpose, Core Values, and Beliefs
    A. Do the superintendent and board accept the belief that 94 to 97 percent of the school district's issues are system problems?

    B. Has the organization disavowed the use of force, intimidation, manipulation, or incentives to achieve its goals?

    C. Does the organization have in place structures to regularly remove barriers and waste?

    D. Do all employees believe their job contributes to the district aim and believe their contribution is valued by their bosses?

II. Constancy of Purpose

    A. Is there an agreed-upon aim for the work of the school district, as a whole, and an aim for every subject and operation?

    B. Are students and employees given freedom to explore alternative ways to accomplish the aim of the system and aim of particular subjects and operations?

    C. Is their evidence that innovation (including technological innovation) solves system problems and helps various divisions meet their aims?

    D. When problems occur, is there a definite process that is always used to solve problems?

The People

III. Development of People

    A. Has the school system calculated the average investment in each employee's personal development over the course of his or her career?

    B. Is there a structure in place for the development of teachers, administrators, support staff, students, and board members?

    C. Is there a structure in place for the development of l eaders—teachers, administrators, support staff, students, and board members?

    D. Is there evidence that the school system's staff development, over the past five years, is having the desired results?

IV. Communication

    A. Are structured listening procedures and time lines in place?

    B. Is communication through evaluation (grades and employee appraisal) assisting the district in meeting its aim?

    C. Does the school district have an established ratio between evaluation and feedback?

    D. Do the regular communications to students, parents, and community provide results of feedback and improvements because of the feedback?

V. Safety

    A. Is baseline data collected on safety?

    B. Is the emergency preparation rehearsed on a regular basis? Is the communication system for crisis management in everyone's mind?

    C. Is there evidence of improved safety in all aspects (physical, sexual, bullying, toxins, psychological)?

    D. Is there evidence of a safer school community and evidence of less expense on safety at the same time?

VI. Personnel Office

    A. Does the district have a structured recruitment/interview/hiring/retention process?

    B. Does the system have an agreed-upon process to build quality and appropriate relationships with all employees?

    C. Does the district have a structured process for documentation of poor performance?

    D. Does the personnel office have a feedback system from employees regarding all aspects of personnel responsibilities?

The Physical Assets

VII. Finance

    A. On every day of every year, do finance, payroll, and personnel have in their databases the exact same number of employees?

    B. Is there a monthly budget synthesis that serves as an early warning system?

    C. Does one person have the overall responsibility for increasing income?

D. Can the district document that fewer resources (time and money) are spent operating the finance system?

VIII. Operations and Buildings

A. Has the school system calculated the cost per pupil for each noninstructional operation?

B. Is each operation testing at least one hypothesis to reduce costs (without reducing quality of service)?

C. Is each operation testing hypotheses to increase quality of service (without increasing costs)?

D. Is there evidence over several years that overall operations have decreased the annual cost per pupil and increased the quality of service?

The Student Learning

IX. Process (Formative) Data

A. Is every student informed on the first day of every course precisely what they will learn in the course?

B. Do teachers and principals receive weekly feedback on learning progress toward meeting end-of-the-year expectations in all classes? Are the three basic classroom graphs (class/student run chart, histogram, and scatter diagram) in place in over 90 percent of the classrooms?

C. Is there a culture of celebrating ATBs (all-time-bests) by student, classroom, grade level, department, and school?

D. Are students and staff actively involved in establishing hypotheses they can test out for the improvement of learning?

X. Results (Summative) Data

A. Are all data reported as a pattern or trend over a minimum of five years?

B. Are the five basic graphs (run, radar, correlation, control chart, and Pareto) used to analyze and communicate all end-of-the-year results data?

C. Is there a culture of celebrating ATBs (all-time-bests) by student, classroom, grade level, department, and school?

      D. Is there a record of increased achievement with a balanced curriculum?

XI. Curriculum

      A. Are over 90 percent of the essential concepts students are to know and be able to do aligned within the school system from kindergarten through grade twelve?

      B. Are the students and parents provided the aligned curriculum documents?

      C. Are students given a common end-of-grade level/course exam?

      D. Has a structure and ratio been established to remove "permission to forget" from prior grade levels and courses?

XII. Instruction

      A. Are standards the foundation for instruction?

      B. Have district staff members agreed upon the ingredients of powerful instruction? Do classroom observations document that these practices are in place over 90 percent of the time?

      C. Are all teachers members of at least one group of peers meeting regularly to study student learning, to agree upon pacing guides, to study item analyses, and to review teaching strategies?

      D. Has the district identified all of the activities that are necessary only because of some instructional failure, and is there a district-created flowchart designed to reduce these failures?

NOTES

1. Senge, 114.
2. Ackoff, 205.

A

PERMISSION FOR INTERDISCIPLINARY ASSIGNMENT

Dust Devils

Santa Cruz Valley Union High School
Permission for Interdisciplinary Assignment

Dust Devils

Student: _____

Courses 1._____   2_____   3._____

Proposed Alternative Assignment

_____

_____

_____

_____

Assignment 1

Teacher: _____   Assignment: _____

Criteria
1. _____
2. _____
3. _____

Assignment 2

Teacher: _____   Assignment: _____

Criteria
1. _____
2. _____
3. _____

Assignment 3

Teacher: _____   Assignment: _____

Criteria
1. _____
2. _____
3. _____

Approvals

_____	_____	_____
Teacher — Assignment 1	Teacher — Assignment 2	Teacher — Assignment 3

Due Date: _____

B

THE KEY PROBLEMS

Key Problem 1: School leaders live and work in a blaming society; blaming solves nothing.

Key Problem 2: Management by objective (MBO) fuels the educational pendulum; schools must move beyond MBO.

Key Problem 3: People development is the business of schools; however, this central task is often left to chance.

Key Problem 4: Schools systems tell in multiple languages; they formally listen in zero languages.

Key Problem 5: Every dollar spent on safety subtracts from money invested in instruction; nevertheless, when safety is at risk nothing else matters.

Key Problem 6: Often no agreed-upon standard exists for hiring or retention of employees; merely filling positions has been the aim far too often.

Key Problem 7: The people ultimately responsible for prudent fiscal management (superintendent and school board) are almost never accountants; key systems are not in place for nonaccountant leaders and thus more and more time is subtracted from instruction and put into finance.

Key Problem 8:   Structures are not in place to increase the quality of noninstructional operations and reduce costs at the same time; most school districts do not have this as the aim of operations.

Key Problem 9:   Today's educators inherited data practices that demoralize all but a few students; statistics must become the friend of both students and the faculty.

Key Problem 10:   Annual data is often used to hammer schools; the real purpose should be to provide insights to create a better future.

Key Problem 11:   The public is paying for thirteen years of K–12 education and receiving eight years of learning; schools spend, on the average, one-third of each year reviewing prior year's curriculum.

Key Problem 12:   Schools have the responsibility to provide students a common experience regardless of teacher assignment and subsequent teacher strengths and interests; neither dictatorship nor laissez-faire management is the solution.

BIBLIOGRAPHY

Ackoff, Russell L. *The Democratic Corporation*. New York: Oxford University Press, 1994.

Berman, Karen, and Joe Knight. *Financial Intelligence*. Boston, MA: Harvard Business School Press, 2006.

Brassard, Michael, and Diane Ritter. *The Memory Jogger for Education*. Methuen, MA: Goal/QPC, 1992.

Buckingham, Marcus. *The One Thing You Need to Know*. New York: Simon and Schuster, 2005.

Burlingham, Bo. *Small Giants*. New York: Portfolio, 2005.

Collins, Jim. *Good to Great*. New York: HarperCollins Publishers, 2001.

Conyers, John. "Charting Your Course: Lessons Learned During the Journey Toward Performance Excellence." Paper presented at the American Society for Quality Leadership Institute, St. Petersburg, FL, June 2004.

Davenport, Patricia, and Gerald Anderson. *Closing the Achievement Gap*. Houston, TX: American Productivity and Quality Center, 2003.

Deci, Edward L., and Richard Flaste. *Why We Do What We Do*. New York: Portfolio, 1996.

Deming, W. Edwards. Address, American Association of School Administrators, Washington, D.C., January 1992.

——.*The New Economics for Industry, Government and Education*. Cambridge, MA: Massachusetts Institute of Technology, Center for Advanced Engineering Study, 1993.

——. *Some Theory of Sampling*. New York: Dover Publications, 1950.

DuFour, Richard, Rebecca DuFour, Robert Eaker, and Gayle Kaharnek. *Whatever It Takes*. Bloomington, IN: Solution Tree, 2004.

Education Policy and Leadership Center K-12 School Leadership Study Group. *Strengthening School Leadership*. Harrisburg, PA: The Education Policy and Leadership Center, 2006.

Freese, Thomas A. *Secrets of Question Based Selling*. Naperville, IL: Sourcebooks, 2000.

Givray, Henry R. "When CEOs Aren't Leaders." *BusinessWeek*, September 3, 2007.

Gladwell, Malcolm. *The Tipping Point*. New York: Little Brown and Co., 2000.

Guiliani, Rudolph W., and Ken Kurson. *Leadership*. New York: Hyperion, 2002.

Guskey, Thomas R., and Jane M. Bailey. *Developing Grading and Reporting Systems for Student Learning*. Experts in Assessment Series. Thousand Oaks, CA: Corwin Press, 2001.

Ha, Warren T., ed. *The Book of Statistical Process Control*. Cincinnati, OH: Zontec, 2002.

Heath, Chip, and Dan Heath. "Success Can Make You Stupid." *Fast Company*, May 2007.

Huckabee, Mike. *From Hope to Higher Ground*. New York: Warner Books, 2007.

Jenkins, Lee, Lloyd O. Roettger, and Caroline Roettger. *Boot Camp for Leaders in K-12 Education: Continuous Improvement*. Milwaukee, WI: Quality Press, 2007.

Jenkins, Lee. *Improving Student Learning: Applying Deming's Quality Principles in Classrooms*. 2nd ed. Milwaukee, WI: Quality Press, 2003.

——. *Permission to Forget: And Nine Other Root Causes of America's Frustration with Education*. Milwaukee, WI: Quality Press, 2005.

Jones, Del. "Toyota's Success Pleases Proponents of 'Lean.'" *USA Today*, May 4, 2007.

Kaplan, Robert S., and David P. Norton. *The Balanced Scorecard*. Boston, MA: Harvard Business School Press, 1996.

Kilian, Cecelia S. *The World of W. Edwards Deming*. Knoxville, TN: SPC Press, 1992.

Latzko, William J., and David Saunders. *Four Days with Dr. Deming*. Reading, MA: Addison-Wesley, 1995.

Liker, Jeffrey K. *The Toyota Way*. New York: McGraw-Hill, 2004.

Lundin, Stephen C., Harry Paul, and John Christensen. *Fish!* New York: Hyperion, 2000.

Maxwell, John C. *The Maxwell Leadership Bible*. Nashville, TN: Thomas Nelson Publishers, 2002.

McGrath, Mary Jo. "The Case of the Messy Desk." *The School Administrator* 64, no. 6, June 2007, 30. Arlington, VA: American Association of School Administrators.

McGregor, Jena. "Most Innovative Companies." *BusinessWeek*, May 14, 2007.

Meterstrom, Kristin. "New York City Educator Pushes Incentives for Teachers." *Arkansas Democrat-Gazette*, May 15, 2007.

Michelli, Joseph A. *The Starbucks Experience*. New York: McGraw-Hill, 2007.

Myra, Harold, and Marshall Shelley. *The Leadership Secrets of Billy Graham*. Grand Rapids, MI: Zondervan Publishers, 2005.

Prospero, Michael A. "NASCAR Car of Tomorrow." *Fast Company*, May 2007.

Reeves, Douglas B. *The Leader's Guide to Standards*. San Francisco: John Wiley and Sons, 2002.

Salter, Chuck. "Failure Doesn't Suck" (interview with Sir James Dyson). *Fast Company*, May 2007, 44.

Schmoker, Michael J. *Results Now*. Alexandria, VA: Association for Supervision and Curriculum Development, 2006.

Senge, Peter M. *The Fifth Discipline*. New York: Currency/Doubleday, 1990.

Shewhart, Walter A. *Statistical Method from the Viewpoint of Quality Control*. Mineola, NY: Dover Press, 1986.

Sieden, Lloyd Steven. *Buckminster Fuller's Universe*. Cambridge, MA: Perseus Publishing, 1989.

Thompson, Michael Clay. *Classics in the Classroom*. Unionville, NY: Royal Fireworks Press, 1995.

Trotter, Andrew. "Major Study on Software Stirs Debate." *Education Week* 26, no. 32, April 11, 2007, 1.

——. "Seeing No Progress Some Schools Drop Laptops." *New York Times*, May 4, 2007.

——. "Glitches in Los Angeles Payroll System Spark Furor." *Education Week* 26, no. 42, June 20, 2007, 1.

Tufte, Edward R. *The Visual Display of Quantitative Information*. 2nd ed. Cheshire, CT: Graphics Press, 2001.

Webber, Larry, and Michael Wallace. *Quality Control for Dummies*. Hoboken, NJ: Wiley Publishing Inc., 2007.

Yazzie-Mintz, Ethan. *Voices of Students on Engagement*. Bloomington, IN: Indiana University School of Education High School Survey of Student Engagement, 2006. http://ceep.indiana.edu/hssse.

INDEX

Ackoff, Russell, 22, 24, 123, 150
aim, xiv, 14, 20–28, 49, 63
alignment 24, 138, 140
all-time best, 116, 132
average, xix, xx, 6, 37, 38, 47, 51, 79, 81, 83, 108, 114, 122, 123, 130, 131, 142, 155

background knowledge, 113, 147–48
balanced curriculum, 133–34
barriers, 12–16, 46, 85
Barth, Roland, 44
bell curve, xix
Bloom's taxonomy, 148
Buckingham, Marcus, 110
budget, 15, 89–95, 103, 151, 154, 166

Carson, Shelly, 58
Cecil County, Maryland, 126
celebration, 11, 116–17, 133
chamber of commerce graph, xx, 124
Collins, Jim, 9, 18, 32, 45, 77, 81
competitive, xv
complaints, 69, 101

continuous improvement, xxi, 112, 117, 124
control chart, xx, 123, 130–32
Conyers, John, 13, 56
cooperation, xv, 113, 117
correlation, xx, 28, 31, 123, 128–29
cost per pupil, 76, 98–102
Cottrell, Vic, 40–42, 79–82
curriculum, xxi, 23, 39, 48, 69, 94, 112, 118, 133–46, 152, 156–58

Deci, Edward, 10, 22, 44, 58, 67
Deming, W. Edwards, ix, xiii, xvi, 4–9, 14–15, 19, 26–27, 32, 39, 47, 51, 57, 66, 95, 131–33, 153
documentation, 41, 83–85
Dover-Eyota School District, Minnesota, 5
DuFour, Richard, 61, 150, 158
Dyson, Sir James, 28, 99

emergency, 59, 74–75
evaluation, 45, 51–52, 64–70, 80, 85, 101, 148, 154–56

exams, xix, 8, 51, 65, 108, 122, 126, 141, 167

failure, xix, 20, 48, 60, 99, 122, 154–58
fear, 9, 11, 15, 84, 90, 99
feedback, 42, 85, 109, 113
Feuerstein, Reuven, 159
flowchart, 154, 158–59
formative data, xix, 67, 107–10, 128, 167
Freese, Thomas A., x, 52
Fuller, Buckminster, 25, 149

geography, 118
Girvay, Henry, 48
Giuliani, Rudolph, 21–22, 123
goals, 7–11, 20, 30–31, 64, 116, 128, 132, 147, 165
grades, xvii, 5, 8, 10, 62–68, 108–10, 147, 155, 167–68
graduation, xvi, 49, 51, 113, 127, 139, 167
Guskey and Bailey, 67, 147

"happy face" survey, 58
Heath, Chip, 133
Heath, Dan, 133
hiring, 77–78, 80–82
histogram, xx, 109, 115–17
hypotheses, xx–xxii, 30, 99–100, 117–18

IEP, 63, 134
improvement, x, xi, xii, xxi, 9, 12–13, 21–22, 26, 28–29, 31–32, 47, 50–51, 58, 66, 68–69, 75, 101, 112, 117–18, 121–33, 150–51
incentives, xvii, 7–12, 14, 123
income, 90–94
interview, 5, 12, 46, 77–81, 102, 110
item analysis, xx, 65–69, 129, 153

Jenks, Oklahoma 99
job description, xiii, 24, 45, 83, 94

Kaplan and Norton, 32, 50, 59, 82, 85, 93, 95, 164
Klein, Joel, 9

leaders, ix, x, xiii, xiv, xv, xvii, xix, xxi, 4–9, 13–16, 25–28, 32, 37–39, 44–50, 59, 85, 91, 97–100, 107–10, 118, 123–24, 128, 131, 134, 152, 163–65
learning communities, 50, 117, 151, 153

management, four generations, xvi, 19, 153
Maxwell, John, 7
Maconaquah School Corporation, 107
McCaulley, Dan 108
McDonald, John, 156
McGrath, Mary Jo, 84
memory, 5, 109–10, 148–49, 154, 159, 168
mistake, xix, 60, 81–82, 95, 131, 134, 152
motivation, xvii, xviii, 10–11, 13, 42, 44, 64, 68, 142

No Child Left Behind, 132
Nordberg, Marion, 62

open-door policy, 83
Otero, Julie, 112
outcomes, 108, 113, 115

pacing guide, 151–53
pareto chart, xx, 31–32, 73–74, 123, 129–30
payroll, 11, 15, 57, 89–91, 97
permission to forget, 5–6, 137, 141–42, 152, 167, 169
PGA, 123
Piaget, Jean, xvii
Pine Island, Minnesota, 73
Plan-Do-Study-Act, xxi, 32
Plus-Delta, 57–58, 68–69

Poffenbarger, Robert, 80, 84, 125
process data. *See* formative data
publishers, 137–38, 145
purchase orders, 94

quality standards, 81–82, 98, 147

radar chart, 31, 123, 125–28
random sampling, 100–101, 154
ranking/ranked, xvii, 62, 122, 130–31
Reeves, Douglas, 154, 157
Reichart, Carl, 95
reflection, 149–50, 164
relationships, xv, 29–30, 41–42, 50,
    60–61, 78–79, 82–83
results, xvi, xix, xx, xxi, 4,6,9, 12,
    22–23, 25, 28, 31, 45, 48–49, 52, 57,
    59, 66, 69, 100, 110, 112, 117, 121–34,
    171
Rhodes, Lew, 29
root cause, xxi, 3–4, 12, 14, 32, 155, 157
run chart, xx, 109–12, 110, 115, 117–18,
    123

safety, 15, 71–76
sample, 57, 65–69, 112, 138
scatter diagram, xx, 114–17, 128
Schmoker, Michael, 108, 110, 113, 127,
    142, 146
Schmook, Michael, 126

Senge, Peter, 4, 25, 48, 57, 62, 81, 113,
    140, 151
Shewhart, Walter, 110, 163
standards, xxii, 23, 62–63, 65, 69, 81–82,
    98, 101, 107–8, 114–15, 122, 125,
    128, 137–38, 140, 145–56, 149–55,
    157
Starbucks, 26, 44, 149
statistical control, xx
suboptimize, xv, 165
support staff, 15, 29, 38, 40–44, 82, 103

team, xvi, 20–21, 82, 92, 108, 116–18,
    125, 133, 140, 150–51, 153–54, 165
technology, 26–30, 59, 94, 147, 150, 158
tenure, 37, 81, 165
Thompson, Michael, 26, 61, 141, 148
Toyota, 9, 13, 21, 28–29, 32, 45, 130, 147

vandalism, 15, 73, 75–76
variation, xiii, xviii–xx, 52, 66, 110, 122,
    128, 130–31

warning, early, 90–91
waste, 12–14, 20, 45, 69, 94–95, 114,
    116, 138, 140, 154
Watkins, Bill, 60
Webber and Wallace, 59, 155, 157
Wilson, Woody, 156
Winter, Sue, 113

ABOUT THE AUTHOR

Lee Jenkins, one of America's most provocative educators, is founder of From LtoJ Consulting Group, Inc., which provides seminars and ongoing assistance to educators. He has addressed both international and U.S. educators in school districts, intermediate service agencies and conferences held by the American Association of School Administrators, the American Society for Quality, and State Departments of Education. Previously Jenkins served as a California district superintendent, principal, curriculum coordinator, and teacher. He has taught part-time for numerous universities and full-time for Oregon State University. He holds a PhD in school leadership/curriculum from The Claremont Graduate University. Jenkins previously authored *Improving Student Learning, Permission to Forget* and coauthored *Boot Camp for Leaders in K–12 Education.* He resides in Scottsdale, Arizona, with his wife, Sandy.